FOREWORD

The collection of "Everything Will Be Okay" travel phrasebooks published by T&P Books is designed for people traveling abroad for tourism and business. The phrasebooks contain what matters most - the essentials for basic communication. This is an indispensable set of phrases to "survive" while abroad.

This phrasebook will help you in most cases where you need to ask something, get directions, find out how much something costs, etc. It can also resolve difficult communication situations where gestures just won't help.

This book contains a lot of phrases that have been grouped according to the most relevant topics. A separate section of the book also provides a small dictionary with more than 1,500 important and useful words.

Take "Everything Will Be Okay" phrasebook with you on the road and you'll have an irreplaceable traveling companion who will help you find your way out of any situation and teach you to not fear speaking with foreigners.

TABLE OF CONTENTS

T&P Books Publishing

Travel phrasebooks collection
«Everything Will Be Okay!»

T&P Books Publishing

PHRASEBOOK
— KOREAN —

THE MOST IMPORTANT PHRASES

This phrasebook contains
the most important
phrases and questions
for basic communication
Everything you need
to survive overseas

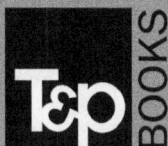

T&P BOOKS

By Andrey Taranov

Phrasebook + 1500-word dictionary

English-Korean phrasebook & concise dictionary

By Andrey Taranov

The collection of "Everything Will Be Okay" travel phrasebooks published by T&P Books is designed for people traveling abroad for tourism and business. The phrasebooks contain what matters most - the essentials for basic communication. This is an indispensable set of phrases to "survive" while abroad.

Another section of the book also provides a small dictionary with more than 1,500 useful words arranged alphabetically. The dictionary includes a lot of gastronomic terms and will be helpful when ordering food at a restaurant or buying groceries at the store.

T&P Books Publishing
www.tpbooks.com

ISBN: 978-1-78616-755-2

This book is also available in E-book formats.
Please visit www.tpbooks.com or the major online bookstores.

PRONUNCIATION

Letter	Korean example	T&P phonetic alphabet	English example

Consonants

Letter	Korean example	T&P phonetic alphabet	English example
ㄱ [1]	개	[k]	clock, kiss
ㄱ [2]	아기	[g]	game, gold
ㄲ	껌	[k]	tense [k]
ㄴ	눈	[n]	name, normal
ㄷ [3]	달	[t]	tourist, trip
ㄷ [4]	사다리	[d]	day, doctor
ㄸ	딸	[t]	tense [t]
ㄹ [5]	라디오	[r]	rice, radio
ㄹ [6]	심팔	[l]	lace, people
ㅁ	문	[m]	magic, milk
ㅂ [7]	봄	[p]	pencil, private
ㅂ [8]	아버지	[b]	baby, book
ㅃ	빵	[p]	tense [p]
ㅅ [9]	실	[s]	city, boss
ㅅ [10]	옷	[t]	tourist, trip
ㅆ	쌀	[ja:]	royal
ㅇ [11]	강	[ŋg]	language, single
ㅈ [12]	집	[tɕ]	cheer
ㅈ [13]	아주	[dʑ]	jeans, gene
ㅉ	짬	[tɕ]	tense [tch]
ㅊ	차	[tʃh]	hitchhiker
ㅌ	택시	[th]	don't have
ㅋ	칼	[kh]	work hard
ㅍ	포도	[ph]	top hat
ㅎ	한국	[h]	home, have

Letter	Korean example	T&P phonetic alphabet	English example

Vowels and combinations with vowels

ㅏ	사	[a]	shorter than in ask
ㅑ	향	[ja]	Kenya, piano
ㅓ	머리	[ʌ]	lucky, sun
ㅕ	병	[jɑ]	young, yard
ㅗ	몸	[o]	pod, John
ㅛ	표	[jɔ]	New York
ㅜ	물	[u]	book
ㅠ	슈퍼	[ju]	youth, usually
ㅡ	음악	[ı]	big, America
ㅣ	길	[i], [i:]	feet, Peter
ㅐ	뱀	[ɛ], [ɛ:]	habit, bad
ㅒ	애기	[je]	yesterday, yen
ㅔ	펜	[e]	elm, medal
ㅖ	계산	[je]	yesterday, yen
ㅘ	왕	[wa]	watt, white
ㅙ	왜	[ʊə]	pure, fuel
ㅚ	회의	[ø], [we]	first, web
ㅝ	권	[uɔ]	to order, to open
ㅞ	웬	[ʊə]	pure, fuel
ㅟ	쥐	[wi]	whiskey
ㅢ	거의	[ɯi]	combination [ıi]

Comments

[1] at the beginning of words
[2] between voiced sounds
[3] at the beginning of words
[4] between voiced sounds
[5] at the beginning of a syllable
[6] at the end of a syllable
[7] at the beginning of words
[8] between voiced sounds
[9] at the beginning of a syllable
[10] at the end of a syllable
[11] at the end of a syllable
[12] at the beginning of words
[13] between voiced sounds

LIST OF ABBREVIATIONS

English abbreviations

ab.	-	about
adj	-	adjective
adv	-	adverb
anim.	-	animate
as adj	-	attributive noun used as adjective
e.g.	-	for example
etc.	-	et cetera
fam.	-	familiar
fem.	-	feminine
form.	-	formal
inanim.	-	inanimate
masc.	-	masculine
math	-	mathematics
mil.	-	military
n	-	noun
pl	-	plural
pron.	-	pronoun
sb	-	somebody
sing.	-	singular
sth	-	something
v aux	-	auxiliary verb
vi	-	intransitive verb
vi, vt	-	intransitive, transitive verb
vt	-	transitive verb

T&P BOOKS

KOREAN
PHRASEBOOK

This section contains
important phrases that may
come in handy in various
real-life situations.
The phrasebook will help
you ask for directions, clarify
a price, buy tickets, and
order food at a restaurant

T&P Books Publishing

PHRASEBOOK
CONTENTS

T&P Books Publishing

The bare minimum

Excuse me, ...	실례합니다, ... sil-lye-ham-ni-da, ...
Hello.	안녕하세요. an-nyeong-ha-se-yo.
Thank you.	감사합니다. gam-sa-ham-ni-da.
Good bye.	안녕히 계세요. an-nyeong-hi gye-se-yo.
Yes.	네. ne.
No.	아니오. a-ni-o.
I don't know.	모르겠어요. mo-reu-ge-seo-yo.
Where? | Where to? | When?	어디예요? | 어디까지 가세요? | 언제요? eo-di-ye-yo? | eo-di-kka-ji ga-se-yo? | eon-je-yo?

I need ...	··· 필요해요. ... pi-ryo-hae-yo.
I want ...	··· 싶어요. ... si-peo-yo.
Do you have ...?	··· 있으세요? ... i-seu-se-yo?
Is there a ... here?	여기 ··· 있어요? yeo-gi ... i-seo-yo?
May I ...?	···해도 되나요? ... hae-do doe-na-yo?
..., please (polite request)	···, 부탁합니다. ..., bu-tak-am-ni-da.

I'm looking for ...	··· 찾고 있어요. ... chat-go i-seo-yo.
restroom	화장실 hwa-jang-sil
ATM	현금인출기 hyeon-geum-in-chul-gi
pharmacy (drugstore)	약국 yak-guk
hospital	병원 byeong-won
police station	경찰서 gyeong-chal-seo

subway	지하철 ji-ha-cheol
taxi	택시 taek-si
train station	기차역 gi-cha-yeok

My name is ...	제 이름은 … 입니다. je i-reu-meun ... im-ni-da.
What's your name?	성함이 어떻게 되세요? seong-ham-i eo-tteo-ke doe-se-yo?
Could you please help me?	도와주세요. do-wa-ju-se-yo.
I've got a problem.	문제가 있어요. mun-je-ga i-seo-yo.
I don't feel well.	몸이 안 좋아요. mom-i an jo-a-yo.
Call an ambulance!	구급차를 불러 주세요! gu-geup-cha-reul bul-leo ju-se-yo!
May I make a call?	전화를 써도 되나요? jeon-hwa-reul sseo-do doe-na-yo?

I'm sorry.	죄송합니다. joe-song-ham-ni-da.
You're welcome.	천만에요. cheon-man-e-yo.

I, me	저 jeo
you (inform.)	너 neo
he	그 geu
she	그녀 geu-nyeo
they (masc.)	그들 geu-deul
they (fem.)	그들 geu-deul
we	우리 u-ri
you (pl)	너희 neo-hui
you (sg, form.)	당신 dang-sin

ENTRANCE	입구 ip-gu
EXIT	출구 chul-gu
OUT OF ORDER	고장 go-jang

CLOSED	닫힘 da-chim
OPEN	열림 yeol-lim
FOR WOMEN	여성용 yeo-seong-yong
FOR MEN	남성용 nam-seong-yong

Questions

Where?	어디예요? eo-di-ye-yo?
Where to?	어디까지 가세요? eo-di-kka-ji ga-se-yo?
Where from?	어디에서요? eo-di-e-seo-yo?
Why?	왜요? wae-yo?
For what reason?	무슨 이유에서요? mu-seun i-yu-e-seo-yo?
When?	언제요? eon-je-yo?
How long?	얼마나요? eol-ma-na-yo?
At what time?	몇 시에요? myeot si-e-yo?
How much?	얼마예요? eol-ma-ye-yo?
Do you have ...?	··· 있으세요? ... i-seu-se-yo?
Where is ...?	··· 어디 있어요? ... eo-di i-seo-yo?
What time is it?	지금 몇 시예요? ji-geum myeot si-ye-yo?
May I make a call?	전화를 써도 되나요? jeon-hwa-reul sseo-do doe-na-yo?
Who's there?	누구세요? nu-gu-se-yo?
Can I smoke here?	담배를 피워도 되나요? dam-bae-reul pi-wo-do doe-na-yo?
May I ...?	··· 되나요? ... doe-na-yo?

Needs

I'd like ...	··· 하고 싶어요.
	... ha-go si-peo-yo.
I don't want ...	··· 하기 싫어요.
	... ha-gi si-reo-yo.
I'm thirsty.	목이 말라요.
	mo-gi mal-la-yo.
I want to sleep.	자고 싶어요.
	ja-go si-peo-yo.

I want ...	··· 싶어요.
	... si-peo-yo.
to wash up	씻고
	ssit-go
to brush my teeth	이를 닦고
	i-reul dak-go
to rest a while	쉬고
	swi-go
to change my clothes	옷을 갈아입고
	os-eul ga-ra-ip-go

to go back to the hotel	호텔로 돌아가고
	ho-tel-lo do-ra-ga-go
to buy ...	··· 사고
	... sa-go
to go to ...	···에 가고
	...e ga-go
to visit ...	···에 방문하고
	...e bang-mun-ha-go
to meet with ...	··· 만나고
	... man-na-go
to make a call	전화를 걸고
	jeon-hwa-reul geol-go

I'm tired.	저는 지쳤어요.
	jeo-neun ji-chyeo-seo-yo.
We are tired.	우리는 지쳤어요.
	u-ri-neun ji-chyeo-seo-yo.
I'm cold.	추워요.
	chu-wo-yo.
I'm hot.	더워요.
	deo-wo-yo.
I'm OK.	괜찮아요.
	gwaen-cha-na-yo.

I need to make a call.

전화를 걸어야 해요.
jeon-hwa-reul geo-reo-ya hae-yo.

I need to go to the restroom.

화장실에 가야 해요.
hwa-jang-si-re ga-ya hae-yo.

I have to go.

가야 해요.
ga-ya hae-yo.

I have to go now.

지금 가야 해요.
ji-geum ga-ya hae-yo.

Asking for directions

Excuse me, ...

실례합니다, ⋯
sil-lye-ham-ni-da, ...

Where is ...?

⋯ 어디 있어요?
... eo-di i-seo-yo?

Which way is ...?

⋯ 어느 쪽이예요?
... eo-neu jjo-gi-ye-yo?

Could you help me, please?

도와주실 수 있어요?
do-wa-ju-sil su i-seo-yo?

I'm looking for ...

⋯ 찾고 있어요.
... chat-go i-seo-yo.

I'm looking for the exit.

출구를 찾고 있어요.
chul-gu-reul chat-go i-seo-yo.

I'm going to ...

⋯에 가고 있어요.
... e ga-go i-seo-yo.

Am I going the right way to ...?

⋯에 가는데 이 길이 맞아요?
...e ga-neun-de i gi-ri ma-ja-yo?

Is it far?

먼가요?
meon-ga-yo?

Can I get there on foot?

걸어갈 수 있어요?
geo-reo-gal su i-seo-yo?

Can you show me on the map?

지도에서 보여주실 수 있어요?
ji-do-e-seo bo-yeo-ju-sil su i-seo-yo?

Show me where we are right now.

지금 우리가 있는 곳을
보여주세요.
ji-geum u-ri-ga in-neun gos-eul
bo-yeo-ju-se-yo.

Here

여기
yeo-gi

There

거기
geo-gi

This way

이 길
i gil

Turn right.

오른쪽으로 가세요.
o-reun-jjo-geu-ro ga-se-yo.

Turn left.

왼쪽으로 가세요.
oen-jjo-geu-ro ga-se-yo.

first (second, third) turn

첫 번째 (두 번째,
세 번째) 골목
cheot beon-jjae (du beon-jjae,
se beon-jjae) gol-mok

to the right	오른쪽으로 o-reun-jjo-geu-ro
to the left	왼쪽으로 oen-jjo-geu-ro
Go straight ahead.	직진하세요. jik-jin-ha-se-yo.

Signs

WELCOME!	환영! hwa-nyeong!
ENTRANCE	입구 ip-gu
EXIT	출구 chul-gu
PUSH	미세요 mi-se-yo
PULL	당기세요 dang-gi-se-yo
OPEN	열림 yeol-lim
CLOSED	닫힘 da-chim
FOR WOMEN	여성용 yeo-seong-yong
FOR MEN	남성용 nam-seong-yong
GENTLEMEN, GENTS (m)	남성 (남) nam-seong (nam)
WOMEN (f)	여성 (여) yeo-seong (yeo)
DISCOUNTS	할인 ha-rin
SALE	세일 se-il
FREE	무료 mu-ryo
NEW!	신상품! sin-sang-pum!
ATTENTION!	주의! ju-ui!
NO VACANCIES	빈 방 없음 bin bang eop-seum
RESERVED	예약석 ye-yak-seok
ADMINISTRATION	사무실 sa-mu-sil
STAFF ONLY	직원 전용 ji-gwon jeo-nyong

BEWARE OF THE DOG!

개조심!
gae-jo-sim!

NO SMOKING!

금연!
geu-myeon!

DO NOT TOUCH!

만지지 마세요!
man-ji-ji ma-se-yo!

DANGEROUS

위험
wi-heom

DANGER

위험
wi-heom

HIGH VOLTAGE

고압 전류
go-ap jeol-lyu

NO SWIMMING!

수영금지!
su-yeong-geum-ji!

OUT OF ORDER

고장
go-jang

FLAMMABLE

가연성
ga-yeon-seong

FORBIDDEN

금지
geum-ji

NO TRESPASSING!

무단횡단 금지
mu-dan-hoeng-dan geum-ji

WET PAINT

젖은 페인트
jeo-jeun pe-in-teu

CLOSED FOR RENOVATIONS

공사중
gong-sa-jung

WORKS AHEAD

전방 공사중
jeon-bang gong-sa-jung

DETOUR

우회 도로
u-hoe do-ro

Transportation. General phrases

plane	비행기 bi-haeng-gi
train	기차 gi-cha
bus	버스 beo-seu
ferry	페리 pe-ri
taxi	택시 taek-si
car	자동차 ja-dong-cha
schedule	시간표 si-gan-pyo
Where can I see the schedule?	시간표는 어디서 볼 수 있어요? si-gan-pyo-neun eo-di-seo bol su i-seo-yo?
workdays (weekdays)	평일 pyeong-il
weekends	주말 ju-mal
holidays	휴일 hyu-il
DEPARTURE	출발 chul-bal
ARRIVAL	도착 do-chak
DELAYED	지연 ji-yeon
CANCELLED	취소 chwi-so
next (train, etc.)	다음 da-eum
first	첫 번째 cheot beon-jjae
last	마지막 ma-ji-mak

When is the next ...?	다음 … 언제인가요? da-eum ... eon-je-in-ga-yo?
When is the first ...?	첫 … 언제인가요? cheot ... eon-je-in-ga-yo?
When is the last ...?	마지막 … 언제인가요? ma-ji-mak ... eon-je-in-ga-yo?

transfer (change of trains, etc.)	환승 hwan-seung
to make a transfer	환승하다 hwan-seung-ha-da
Do I need to make a transfer?	환승해야 해요? hwan-seung-hae-ya hae-yo?

Buying tickets

Where can I buy tickets?	표는 어디서 사나요? pyo-neun eo-di-seo sa-na-yo?
ticket	표 pyo
to buy a ticket	표를 사다 pyo-reul sa-da
ticket price	표 가격 pyo ga-gyeok
Where to?	어디까지 가세요? eo-di-kka-ji ga-se-yo?
To what station?	어느 역까지 가세요? eo-neu yeok-kka-ji ga-se-yo?
I need ...	··· 필요해요. ... pi-ryo-hae-yo.
one ticket	표 한 장 pyo han jang
two tickets	표 두 장 pyo du jang
three tickets	표 세 장 pyo se jang
one-way	편도 pyeon-do
round-trip	왕복 wang-bok
first class	일등석 il-deung-seok
second class	이등석 i-deung-seok
today	오늘 o-neul
tomorrow	내일 nae-il
the day after tomorrow	모레 mo-re
in the morning	아침에 a-chim-e
in the afternoon	오후에 o-hu-e
in the evening	저녁에 jeo-nyeo-ge

aisle seat	복도 좌석 bok-do jwa-seok
window seat	창가 좌석 chang-ga jwa-seok
How much?	얼마예요? eol-ma-ye-yo?
Can I pay by credit card?	신용카드 돼요? si-nyong-ka-deu dwae-yo?

Bus

bus	버스 beo-seu
intercity bus	시외버스 si-oe-beo-seu
bus stop	버스 정류장 beo-seu jeong-nyu-jang
Where's the nearest bus stop?	가까운 버스 정류장이 어디예요? ga-kka-un beo-seu jeong-nyu-jang-i eo-di-ye-yo?
number (bus ~, etc.)	번호 beon-ho
Which bus do I take to get to …?	…에 가려면 어느 버스를 타야 해요? … e ga-ryeo-myeon eo-neu beo-seu-reul ta-ya hae-yo?
Does this bus go to …?	이 버스 … 가요? i beo-seu … ga-yo?
How frequent are the buses?	버스는 얼마나 자주 와요? beo-seu-neun eol-ma-na ja-ju wa-yo?
every 15 minutes	십오 분 마다 si-bo bun ma-da
every half hour	삼십 분 마다 sam-sip bun ma-da
every hour	한 시간 마다 han si-gan ma-da
several times a day	하루에 여러 번 ha-ru-e yeo-reo beon
… times a day	하루에 …번 ha-ru-e …beon
schedule	시간표 si-gan-pyo
Where can I see the schedule?	시간표는 어디서 볼 수 있어요? si-gan-pyo-neun eo-di-seo bol su i-seo-yo?
When is the next bus?	다음 버스는 언제인가요? da-eum beo-seu-neun eon-je-in-ga-yo?
When is the first bus?	첫 버스는 언제인가요? cheot beo-seu-neun eon-je-in-ga-yo?

When is the last bus?	마지막 버스는 언제인가요? ma-ji-mak beo-seu-neun eon-je-in-ga-yo?
stop	정류장 jeong-nyu-jang
next stop	다음 정류장 da-eum jeong-nyu-jang
last stop (terminus)	종점 jong-jeom
Stop here, please.	여기에 세워 주세요. yeo-gi-e se-wo ju-se-yo.
Excuse me, this is my stop.	실례합니다, 저 여기서 내려요. sil-lye-ham-ni-da, jeo yeo-gi-seo nae-ryeo-yo.

Train

train	기차 gi-cha
suburban train	교외 전차 gyo-oe jeon-cha
long-distance train	장거리 기차 jang-geo-ri gi-cha
train station	기차역 gi-cha-yeok
Excuse me, where is the exit to the platform?	실례합니다, 플랫폼으로 가는 출구가 어디인가요? sil-lye-ham-ni-da, peul-laet-po-meu-ro ga-neun chul-gu-ga eo-di-in-ga-yo?

Does this train go to ...?	이 기차 …에 가요? i gi-cha ...e ga-yo?
next train	다음 기차 da-eum gi-cha
When is the next train?	다음 기차는 언제인가요? da-eum gi-cha-neun eon-je-in-ga-yo?
Where can I see the schedule?	시간표는 어디서 볼 수 있어요? si-gan-pyo-neun eo-di-seo bol su i-seo-yo?
From which platform?	어느 플랫폼에서 출발해요? eo-neu peul-laet-pom-e-seo chul-bal-hae-yo?
When does the train arrive in ...?	기차가 …에 언제 도착해요? gi-cha-ga ...e eon-je do-chak-ae-yo?

Please help me.	도와주세요. do-wa-ju-se-yo.
I'm looking for my seat.	제 좌석을 찾고 있어요. je jwa-seo-geul chat-go i-seo-yo.
We're looking for our seats.	우리 좌석을 찾고 있어요. u-ri jwa-seo-geul chat-go i-seo-yo.

My seat is taken.	제 좌석에 다른 사람이 있어요. je jwa-seo-ge da-reun sa-ram-i i-seo-yo.
Our seats are taken.	우리 좌석에 다른 사람이 있어요. u-ri jwa-seo-ge da-reun sa-ram-i i-seo-yo.

I'm sorry but this is my seat.	죄송하지만 여긴 제 좌석이에요. joe-song-ha-ji-man nyeo-gin je jwa-seo-gi-ye-yo.
Is this seat taken?	이 좌석 비었나요? i jwa-seok bi-eon-na-yo?
May I sit here?	여기 앉아도 되나요? yeo-gi an-ja-do doe-na-yo?

On the train. Dialogue (No ticket)

Ticket, please.
표 보여주세요.
pyo bo-yeo-ju-se-yo.

I don't have a ticket.
표가 없어요.
pyo-ga eop-seo-yo.

I lost my ticket.
표를 잃어버렸어요.
pyo-reul ri-reo-beo-ryeo-seo-yo.

I forgot my ticket at home.
표를 집에 두고 왔어요.
pyo-reul ji-be du-go wa-seo-yo.

You can buy a ticket from me.
저한테 표를 사실 수 있어요.
jeo-han-te pyo-reul sa-sil su i-seo-yo.

You will also have to pay a fine.
벌금도 내셔야 해요.
beol-geum-do nae-syeo-ya hae-yo.

Okay.
알았어요.
a-ra-seo-yo.

Where are you going?
어디까지 가세요?
eo-di-kka-ji ga-se-yo?

I'm going to ...
···에 가고 있어요.
... e ga-go i-seo-yo.

How much? I don't understand.
얼마예요? 못 알아들었어요.
eol-ma-ye-yo? mot a-ra-deu-reo-seo-yo.

Write it down, please.
적어 주세요.
jeo-geo ju-se-yo.

Okay. Can I pay with a credit card?
알았어요. 신용카드 돼요?
a-ra-seo-yo. si-nyong-ka-deu dwae-yo?

Yes, you can.
네, 돼요.
ne, dwae-yo.

Here's your receipt.
영수증 여기 있어요.
yeong-su-jeung yeo-gi i-seo-yo.

Sorry about the fine.
벌금을 내게 되어서
유감이예요.
beol-geu-meul lae-ge doe-eo-seo
yu-gam-i-ye-yo.

That's okay. It was my fault.
괜찮아요. 제 잘못이예요.
gwaen-cha-na-yo. je jal-mo-si-ye-yo.

Enjoy your trip.
즐거운 여행 되세요.
jeul-geo-un nyeo-haeng doe-se-yo.

Taxi

taxi	택시 taek-si
taxi driver	택시 운전사 taek-si un-jeon-sa
to catch a taxi	택시를 잡다 taek-si-reul jap-da
taxi stand	택시 정류장 taek-si jeong-nyu-jang
Where can I get a taxi?	어디서 택시를 탈 수 있어요? eo-di-seo taek-si-reul tal su i-seo-yo?
to call a taxi	택시를 부르다. taek-si-reul bu-reu-da.
I need a taxi.	택시가 필요해요. taek-si-ga pi-ryo-hae-yo.
Right now.	지금 당장. ji-geum dang-jang.
What is your address (location)?	주소가 어디예요? ju-so-ga eo-di-ye-yo?
My address is ...	제 주소는 …예요. je ju-so-neun ...ye-yo.
Your destination?	목적지가 어디예요? mok-jeok-ji-ga eo-di-ye-yo?
Excuse me, ...	실례합니다, … sil-lye-ham-ni-da, ...
Are you available?	타도 돼요? ta-do dwae-yo?
How much is it to get to ...?	…까지 얼마예요? ...kka-ji eol-ma-ye-yo?
Do you know where it is?	여기가 어딘지 아세요? yeo-gi-ga eo-din-ji a-se-yo?
Airport, please.	공항까지 가 주세요. gong-hang-kka-ji ga ju-se-yo.
Stop here, please.	여기에 세워 주세요. yeo-gi-e se-wo ju-se-yo.
It's not here.	여기가 아니예요. yeo-gi-ga a-ni-ye-yo.
This is the wrong address.	잘못된 주소예요. jal-mot-doen ju-so-ye-yo.
Turn left.	왼쪽으로 가세요. oen-jjo-geu-ro ga-se-yo.

Turn right.

오른쪽으로 가세요.
o-reun-jjo-geu-ro ga-se-yo.

How much do I owe you?

얼마 내야 해요?
eol-ma nae-ya hae-yo?

I'd like a receipt, please.

영수증 주세요.
yeong-su-jeung ju-se-yo.

Keep the change.

잔돈은 가지세요.
jan-do-neun ga-ji-se-yo.

Would you please wait for me?

기다려 주시겠어요?
gi-da-ryeo ju-si-ge-seo-yo?

five minutes

오분
o-bun

ten minutes

십분
sip-bun

fifteen minutes

십오 분
si-bo bun

twenty minutes

이십분
i-sip-bun

half an hour

삼십분
sam-sip bun

Hotel

Hello.	안녕하세요. an-nyeong-ha-se-yo.
My name is ...	제 이름은 ··· 입니다. je i-reu-meun ... im-ni-da.
I have a reservation.	예약했어요. ye-yak-ae-seo-yo.
I need ...	··· 필요해요. ... pi-ryo-hae-yo.
a single room	싱글 룸 하나 sing-geul lum ha-na
a double room	더블 룸 하나 deo-beul lum ha-na
How much is that?	저건 얼마예요? jeo-geon eol-ma-ye-yo?
That's a bit expensive.	그건 조금 비싸요. geu-geon jo-geum bi-ssa-yo.
Do you have anything else?	다른 옵션 있어요? da-reun op-syeon i-seo-yo?
I'll take it.	그걸로 할게요. geu-geol-lo hal-ge-yo.
I'll pay in cash.	현금으로 낼게요. hyeon-geu-meu-ro nael-ge-yo.
I've got a problem.	문제가 있어요. mun-je-ga i-seo-yo
My ... is broken.	제 ··· 망가졌어요. je ... mang-ga-jyeo-seo-yo.
My ... is out of order.	제 ··· 고장났어요. je ... go-jang-na-seo-yo.
TV	텔레비전 tel-le-bi-jeon
air conditioner	에어컨 e-eo-keon
tap	수도꼭지 su-do-kkok-ji
shower	샤워기 sya-wo-gi
sink	세면대 se-myeon-dae
safe	금고 geum-go

door lock	도어락 do-eo-rak
electrical outlet	콘센트 kon-sen-teu
hairdryer	헤어 드라이어 he-eo deu-ra-i-eo

I don't have ...	… 안 나와요. … an na-wa-yo.
water	물 mul
light	전등 jeon-deung
electricity	전기 jeon-gi

Can you give me ...?	… 주실 수 있어요? … ju-sil su i-seo-yo?
a towel	수건 su-geon
a blanket	담요 da-myo
slippers	슬리퍼 seul-li-peo
a robe	가운 ga-un
shampoo	샴푸 syam-pu
soap	비누 bi-nu

I'd like to change rooms.	방을 바꾸고 싶어요. bang-eul ba-kku-go si-peo-yo.
I can't find my key.	열쇠를 못 찾겠어요. yeol-soe-reul mot chat-ge-seo-yo.
Could you open my room, please?	제 방 문을 열어주실 수 있어요? je bang mu-neul ryeo-reo-ju-sil su i-seo-yo?

Who's there?	누구세요? nu-gu-se-yo?
Come in!	들어오세요! deu-reo-o-se-yo!
Just a minute!	잠깐만요! jam-kkan-ma-nyo!

Not right now, please.	지금 당장은 안돼요. ji-geum dang-jang-eun an-dwae-yo.
Come to my room, please.	제 방으로 와 주세요. je bang-eu-ro wa ju-se-yo.

I'd like to order food service.	룸서비스를 받고 싶어요. rum-seo-bi-seu-reul bat-go si-peo-yo.
My room number is …	제 방 번호는 …예요. je bang beon-ho-neun …ye-yo.
I'm leaving …	저는 …에 떠나요. jeo-neun … e tteo-na-yo.
We're leaving …	우리는 …에 떠나요. u-ri-neun …e tteo-na-yo.
right now	지금 당장 ji-geum dang-jang
this afternoon	오늘 오후 o-neul ro-hu
tonight	오늘밤 o-neul-bam
tomorrow	내일 nae-il
tomorrow morning	내일 아침 nae-il ra-chim
tomorrow evening	내일 저녁 nae-il jeo-nyeok
the day after tomorrow	모레 mo-re

I'd like to pay.	계산하고 싶어요. gye-san-ha-go si-peo-yo.
Everything was wonderful.	전부 다 아주 좋았어요. jeon-bu da a-ju jo-a-seo-yo.
Where can I get a taxi?	어디서 택시를 탈 수 있어요? eo-di-seo taek-si-reul tal su i-seo-yo?
Would you call a taxi for me, please?	택시 불러주실 수 있어요? taek-si bul-leo-ju-sil su i-seo-yo?

Restaurant

Can I look at the menu, please?	메뉴판 볼 수 있어요? me-nyu-pan bol su i-seo-yo?
Table for one.	한 명이요. han myeong-i-yo.
There are two (three, four) of us.	두 (세, 네) 명이요. du (se, ne) myeong-i-yo.

Smoking	흡연 heu-byeon
No smoking	금연 geu-myeon
Excuse me! (addressing a waiter)	저기요! jeo-gi-yo!
menu	메뉴판 me-nyu-pan
wine list	와인 리스트 wa-in li-seu-teu
The menu, please.	메뉴판 주세요. me-nyu-pan ju-se-yo.

Are you ready to order?	주문하시겠어요? ju-mun-ha-si-ge-seo-yo?
What will you have?	어떤 걸로 하시겠어요? eo-tteon geol-lo ha-si-ge-seo-yo?
I'll have ...	저는 … 할게요. jeo-neun ... hal-ge-yo.

I'm a vegetarian.	저는 채식주의자예요. jeo-neun chae-sik-ju-ui-ja-ye-yo.
meat	고기 go-gi
fish	생선 saeng-seon
vegetables	채소 chae-so

Do you have vegetarian dishes?	채식 메뉴 있어요? chae-sik me-nyu i-seo-yo?
I don't eat pork.	돼지고기 못 먹어요. dwae-ji-go-gi mot meo-geo-yo.
He /she/ doesn't eat meat.	그는 /그녀는/ 고기 못 드세요. geu-neun /geu-nyeo-neun/ go-gi mot deu-se-yo.

I am allergic to ...

저 …에 알러지 있어요.
jeo ...e al-leo-ji i-seo-yo.

Would you please bring me ...

… 가져다 주시겠어요?
... ga-jyeo-da ju-si-ge-seo-yo?

salt | pepper | sugar

소금 | 후추 | 설탕
so-geum | hu-chu | seol-tang

coffee | tea | dessert

커피 | 차 | 디저트
keo-pi | cha | di-jeo-teu

water | sparkling | plain

물 | 탄산수 | 생수
mul | tan-san-su | saeng-su

a spoon | fork | knife

숟가락 | 포크 | 나이프
sut-ga-rak | po-keu | na-i-peu

a plate | napkin

앞접시 | 휴지
ap-jeop-si | hyu-ji

Enjoy your meal!

맛있게 드세요!
man-nit-ge deu-se-yo!

One more, please.

하나 더 주세요.
ha-na deo ju-se-yo.

It was very delicious.

아주 맛있었어요.
a-ju man-ni-seo-seo-yo.

---

check | change | tip

계산서 | 거스름돈 | 팁
gye-san-seo | geo-seu-reum-don | tip

Check, please.
(Could I have the check, please?)

계산서 주세요.
gye-san-seo ju-se-yo.

Can I pay by credit card?

신용카드 돼요?
si-nyong-ka-deu dwae-yo?

I'm sorry, there's a mistake here.

죄송한데 여기
잘못됐어요.
joe-song-han-de yeo-gi
jal-mot-dwae-seo-yo.

Shopping

Can I help you?	도와드릴까요? do-wa-deu-ril-kka-yo?
Do you have ...?	… 있으세요? ... i-seu-se-yo?
I'm looking for ...	… 찾고 있어요. ... chat-go i-seo-yo.
I need ...	… 필요해요. ... pi-ryo-hae-yo.
I'm just looking.	그냥 구경중이예요. geu-nyang gu-gyeong-jung-i-ye-yo.
We're just looking.	우리 그냥 구경중이예요. u-ri geu-nyang gu-gyeong-jung-i-ye-yo.
I'll come back later.	나중에 다시 올게요. na-jung-e da-si ol-ge-yo.
We'll come back later.	우리 나중에 다시 올게요. u-ri na-jung-e da-si ol-ge-yo.
discounts	sale	할인	세일 ha-rin	se-il
Would you please show me ...	… 보여주세요. ... bo-yeo-ju-se-yo.
Would you please give me ...	… 주세요. ... ju-se-yo.
Can I try it on?	입어봐도 돼요? i-beo-bwa-do dwae-yo?
Excuse me, where's the fitting room?	실례합니다, 피팅 룸 어디 있어요? sil-lye-ham-ni-da, pi-ting num eo-di i-seo-yo?
Which color would you like?	다른 색도 있어요? da-reun saek-do i-seo-yo?
size	length	사이즈	길이 sa-i-jeu	gi-ri
How does it fit?	이거 저한테 맞아요? i-geo jeo-han-te ma-ja-yo?
How much is it?	얼마예요? eol-ma-ye-yo?
That's too expensive.	너무 비싸요. neo-mu bi-ssa-yo.
I'll take it.	그걸로 할게요. geu-geol-lo hal-ge-yo.

Excuse me, where do I pay?	실례합니다, 계산 어디서 해요?
	sil-lye-ham-ni-da, gye-san eo-di-seo hae-yo?
Will you pay in cash or credit card?	현금으로 하시겠어요 카드로 하시겠어요?
	hyeon-geu-meu-ro ha-si-ge-seo-yo ka-deu-ro ha-si-ge-seo-yo?
In cash | with credit card	현금으로요 | 카드로요
	hyeon-geu-meu-ro-yo | ka-deu-ro-yo

Do you want the receipt?	영수증 드릴까요?
	yeong-su-jeung deu-ril-kka-yo?
Yes, please.	네, 주세요.
	ne, ju-se-yo.
No, it's OK.	아니오, 괜찮아요.
	a-ni-o, gwaen-cha-na-yo.
Thank you. Have a nice day!	감사합니다. 즐거운 하루 되세요!
	gam-sa-ham-ni-da. jeul-geo-un ha-ru doe-se-yo!

In town

Excuse me, please.	실례합니다, 저기요. sil-lye-ham-ni-da, jeo-gi-yo.
I'm looking for ...	··· 찾고 있어요. ... chat-go i-seo-yo.
the subway	지하철 ji-ha-cheol
my hotel	제 호텔 je ho-tel
the movie theater	영화관 yeong-hwa-gwan
a taxi stand	택시 정류장 taek-si jeong-nyu-jang

an ATM	현금인출기 hyeon-geum-in-chul-gi
a foreign exchange office	환전소 hwan-jeon-so
an internet café	피씨방 pi-ssi-bang
... street	···로 ...ro
this place	여기 yeo-gi

Do you know where ... is?	··· 어디인지 아세요? ... eo-di-in-ji a-se-yo?
Which street is this?	여기가 어디예요? yeo-gi-ga eo-di-ye-yo?
Show me where we are right now.	지금 우리가 있는 곳을 보여주세요. ji-geum u-ri-ga in-neun gos-eul bo-yeo-ju-se-yo.
Can I get there on foot?	걸어갈 수 있어요? geo-reo-gal su i-seo-yo?
Do you have a map of the city?	시내 지도 있어요? si-nae ji-do i-seo-yo?

How much is a ticket to get in?	입장권 얼마예요? ip-jang-gwon eol-ma-ye-yo?
Can I take pictures here?	사진 찍어도 돼요? sa-jin jji-geo-do dwae-yo?
Are you open?	열었어요? yeo-reo-seo-yo?

When do you open?

언제 열어요?
eon-je yeo-reo-yo?

When do you close?

언제 닫아요?
eon-je da-da-yo?

Money

money	돈 don
cash	현금 hyeon-geum
paper money	지폐 ji-pye
loose change	동전 dong-jeon
check | change | tip	계산서 | 거스름돈 | 팁 gye-san-seo | geo-seu-reum-don | tip
credit card	카드 ka-deu
wallet	지갑 ji-gap
to buy	사다 sa-da
to pay	내다 nae-da
fine	벌금 beol-geum
free	무료 mu-ryo
Where can I buy ...?	··· 어디서 살 수 있어요? ... eo-di-seo sal su i-seo-yo?
Is the bank open now?	은행 지금 열었어요? eun-haeng ji-geum myeo-reo-seo-yo?
When does it open?	언제 열어요? eon-je yeo-reo-yo?
When does it close?	언제 닫아요? eon-je da-da-yo?
How much?	얼마예요? eol-ma-ye-yo?
How much is this?	이건 얼마예요? i-geon eol-ma-ye-yo?
That's too expensive.	너무 비싸요. neo-mu bi-ssa-yo.
Excuse me, where do I pay?	실례합니다, 계산 어디서 해요? sil-lye-ham-ni-da, gye-san eo-di-seo hae-yo?

Check, please.
계산서 주세요.
gye-san-seo ju-se-yo.

Can I pay by credit card?
신용카드 돼요?
si-nyong-ka-deu dwae-yo?

Is there an ATM here?
여기 현금인출기 있어요?
yeo-gi hyeon-geum-in-chul-gi i-seo-yo?

I'm looking for an ATM.
현금 인출기를 찾고
있어요.
hyeon-geum in-chul-gi-reul chat-go
i-seo-yo.

I'm looking for a foreign exchange office.
환전소 찾고 있어요.
hwan-jeon-so chat-go i-seo-yo.

I'd like to change ...
··· 환전하고 싶어요.
... hwan-jeon-ha-go si-peo-yo.

What is the exchange rate?
환율 얼마예요?
hwa-nyul reol-ma-ye-yo?

Do you need my passport?
여권 필요해요?
yeo-gwon pi-ryo-hae-yo?

Time

What time is it?	지금 몇 시예요? ji-geum myeot si-ye-yo?
When?	언제요? eon-je-yo?
At what time?	몇 시에요? myeot si-e-yo?
now | later | after …	지금 | 나중에 | … 이후에 ji-geum | na-jung-e | … i-hu-e
one o'clock	한 시 han si
one fifteen	한 시 십오 분 han si si-bo bun
one thirty	한 시 삼십 분 han si sam-sip bun
one forty-five	한 시 사십오 분 han si sa-si-bo bun

one | two | three	한 | 두 | 세 han | du | se
four | five | six	네 | 다섯 | 여섯 ne | da-seot | yeo-seot
seven | eight | nine	일곱 | 여덟 | 아홉 il-gop | yeo-deol | a-hop
ten | eleven | twelve	열 | 열한 | 열두 yeol | yeol-han | yeol-du

in …	… 안에 … an-e
five minutes	오분 o-bun
ten minutes	십분 sip-bun
fifteen minutes	십오분 si-bo bun
twenty minutes	이십분 i-sip-bun
half an hour	삼십분 sam-sip bun
an hour	한 시간 han si-gan
in the morning	아침에 a-chim-e
early in the morning	아침 일찍 a-chim il-jjik

this morning	오늘 아침 o-neul ra-chim
tomorrow morning	내일 아침 nae-il ra-chim

in the middle of the day	한낮에 han-na-je
in the afternoon	오후에 o-hu-e
in the evening	저녁에 jeo-nyeo-ge
tonight	오늘밤 o-neul-bam

at night	밤에 bam-e
yesterday	어제 eo-je
today	오늘 o-neul
tomorrow	내일 nae-il
the day after tomorrow	모레 mo-re

What day is it today?	오늘이 무슨 요일이예요? o-neu-ri mu-seun nyo-i-ri-ye-yo?
It's ...	··· 예요. ... ye-yo.
Monday	월요일 wo-ryo-il
Tuesday	화요일 hwa-yo-il
Wednesday	수요일 su-yo-il

Thursday	목요일 mo-gyo-il
Friday	금요일 geu-myo-il
Saturday	토요일 to-yo-il
Sunday	일요일 i-ryo-il

Greetings. Introductions

Hello.	안녕하세요. an-nyeong-ha-se-yo.
Pleased to meet you.	만나서 기쁩니다. man-na-seo gi-ppeum-ni-da.
Me too.	저도요. jeo-do-yo.
I'd like you to meet ...	⋯ 소개합니다. ... so-gae-ham-ni-da.
Nice to meet you.	만나서 반갑습니다. man-na-seo ban-gap-seum-ni-da.
How are you?	잘 지내셨어요? jal ji-nae-syeo-seo-yo?
My name is ...	제 이름은 ⋯ 입니다. je i-reu-meun ... im-ni-da.
His name is ...	그의 이름은 ⋯ 예요. geu-ui i-reu-meun ... ye-yo.
Her name is ...	그녀의 이름은 ⋯ 예요. geu-nyeo-ui i-reu-meun ... ye-yo.
What's your name?	성함이 어떻게 되세요? seong-ham-i eo-tteo-ke doe-se-yo?
What's his name?	그분 성함이 뭐예요? geu-bun seong-ham-i mwo-ye-yo?
What's her name?	그분 성함이 뭐예요? geu-bun seong-ham-i mwo-ye-yo?
What's your last name?	성이 어떻게 되세요? seong-i eo-tteo-ke doe-se-yo?
You can call me ...	⋯ 라고 불러 주세요. ... ra-go bul-leo ju-se-yo.
Where are you from?	어디서 오셨어요? eo-di-seo o-syeo-seo-yo?
I'm from ...	⋯ 에서 왔어요. ... e-seo wa-seo-yo.
What do you do for a living?	무슨 일 하세요? mu-seun il ha-se-yo?
Who is this?	이 분은 누구세요? i bu-neun nu-gu-se-yo?
Who is he?	그 분은 누구세요? geu bu-neun nu-gu-se-yo?
Who is she?	그 분은 누구세요? geu bu-neun nu-gu-se-yo?

Who are they?	그 분들은 누구세요? geu bun-deu-reun nu-gu-se-yo?
This is ...	이 쪽은 … 예요. i jjo-geun ... ye-yo.
my friend (masc.)	제 친구 je chin-gu
my friend (fem.)	제 친구 je chin-gu
my husband	제 남편 je nam-pyeon
my wife	제 아내 je a-nae

my father	제 아버지 je a-beo-ji
my mother	제 어머니 je eo-meo-ni
my son	제 아들 je a-deul
my daughter	제 딸 je ttal

This is our son.	이 쪽은 우리 아들이예요. i jjo-geun u-ri a-deu-ri-ye-yo.
This is our daughter.	이 쪽은 우리 딸이예요. i jjo-geun u-ri tta-ri-ye-yo.
These are my children.	이 쪽은 제 아이들이예요. i jjo-geun je a-i-deu-ri-ye-yo.
These are our children.	이 쪽은 우리 아이들이예요. i jjo-geun u-ri a-i-deu-ri-ye-yo.

Farewells

Good bye!
안녕히 계세요!
an-nyeong-hi gye-se-yo!

Bye! (inform.)
안녕!
an-nyeong!

See you tomorrow.
내일 만나요.
nae-il man-na-yo.

See you soon.
곧 만나요.
got man-na-yo.

See you at seven.
일곱 시에 만나요.
il-gop si-e man-na-yo.

Have fun!
재밌게 놀아!
jae-mit-ge no-ra!

Talk to you later.
나중에 봐.
na-jung-e bwa.

Have a nice weekend.
주말 잘 보내.
ju-mal jal bo-nae.

Good night.
안녕히 주무세요.
an-nyeong-hi ju-mu-se-yo.

It's time for me to go.
갈 시간이예요.
gal si-gan-i-ye-yo.

I have to go.
가야 해요.
ga-ya hae-yo.

I will be right back.
금방 다시 올게요.
geum-bang da-si ol-ge-yo.

It's late.
늦었어요.
neu-jeo-seo-yo.

I have to get up early.
일찍 일어나야 해요.
il-jjik gi-reo-na-ya hae-yo.

I'm leaving tomorrow.
내일 떠나요.
nae-il tteo-na-yo.

We're leaving tomorrow.
우리는 내일 떠나요.
u-ri-neun nae-il tteo-na-yo.

Have a nice trip!
즐거운 여행 되세요!
jeul-geo-un nyeo-haeng doe-se-yo!

It was nice meeting you.
만나서 반가웠어요.
man-na-seo ban-ga-wo-seo-yo.

It was nice talking to you.
이야기하느라 즐거웠어요.
i-ya-gi-ha-neu-ra jeul-geo-wo-seo-yo.

Thanks for everything.
전부 다 감사합니다.
jeon-bu da gam-sa-ham-ni-da.

I had a very good time.

아주 즐거웠어요.
a-ju jeul-geo-wo-seo-yo.

We had a very good time.

우리는 아주 즐거웠어요.
u-ri-neun a-ju jeul-geo-wo-seo-yo.

It was really great.

정말 멋졌어요.
jeong-mal meot-jyeo-seo-yo.

I'm going to miss you.

보고 싶을 거예요.
bo-go si-peul geo-ye-yo.

We're going to miss you.

우리는 당신이 보고 싶을
거예요.
u-ri-neun dang-sin-i bo-go si-peul
geo-ye-yo.

Good luck!

행운을 빌어!
haeng-u-neul bi-reo!

Say hi to ...

··· 에게 안부 전해 주세요.
... e-ge an-bu jeon-hae ju-se-yo.

Foreign language

I don't understand.	못 알아들었어요. mot a-ra-deu-reo-seo-yo.
Write it down, please.	적어 주세요. jeo-geo ju-se-yo.
Do you speak ...?	··· 하실 수 있어요? ... ha-sil su i-seo-yo?

| I speak a little bit of ... | 저는 ··· 조금 할 수 있어요.
jeo-neun ... jo-geum hal su i-seo-yo. |
| English | 영어
yeong-eo |

Turkish	터키어 teo-ki-eo
Arabic	아랍어 a-ra-beo
French	프랑스어 peu-rang-seu-eo

German	독일어 do-gi-reo
Italian	이탈리아어 i-tal-li-a-eo
Spanish	스페인어 seu-pe-in-eo

Portuguese	포르투갈어 po-reu-tu-ga-reo
Chinese	중국어 jung-gu-geo
Japanese	일본어 il-bon-eo

Can you repeat that, please.	다시 한 번 말해 주세요. da-si han beon mal-hae ju-se-yo.
I understand.	알아들었어요. a-ra-deu-reo-seo-yo.
I don't understand.	못 알아들었어요. mot a-ra-deu-reo-seo-yo.
Please speak more slowly.	좀 더 천천히 말해 주세요. jom deo cheon-cheon-hi mal-hae ju-se-yo.

Is that correct? (Am I saying it right?)	이거 맞아요? i-geo ma-ja-yo?
What is this? (What does this mean?)	이게 뭐예요? i-ge mwo-ye-yo?

Apologies

Excuse me, please.	실례합니다, 저기요. sil-lye-ham-ni-da, jeo-gi-yo.
I'm sorry.	죄송합니다. joe-song-ham-ni-da.
I'm really sorry.	정말 죄송합니다. jeong-mal joe-song-ham-ni-da.
Sorry, it's my fault.	죄송해요, 제 잘못이에요. joe-song-hae-yo, je jal-mo-si-ye-yo.
My mistake.	제 실수예요. je sil-su-ye-yo.
May I ...?	…해도 되나요? ... hae-do doe-na-yo?
Do you mind if I ...?	…해도 괜찮으세요? ...hae-do gwaen-cha-neu-se-yo?
It's OK.	괜찮아요. gwaen-cha-na-yo.
It's all right.	괜찮아요. gwaen-cha-na-yo.
Don't worry about it.	걱정하지 마세요. geok-jeong-ha-ji ma-se-yo.

Agreement

Yes.
네.
ne.

Yes, sure.
네, 물론입니다.
ne, mul-lon-im-ni-da.

OK (Good!)
좋아요.
jo-a-yo.

Very well.
아주 좋아요.
a-ju jo-a-yo.

Certainly!
당연합니다!
dang-yeon-ham-ni-da!

I agree.
동의해요.
dong-ui-hae-yo.

That's correct.
정확해요.
jeong-hwak-ae-yo.

That's right.
그게 맞아요.
geu-ge ma-ja-yo.

You're right.
당신이 맞아요.
dang-sin-i ma-ja-yo.

I don't mind.
저는 신경 쓰지 않아요.
jeo-neun sin-gyeong sseu-ji a-na-yo.

Absolutely right.
확실히 맞아요.
hwak-sil-hi ma-ja-yo.

It's possible.
가능해요.
ga-neung-hae-yo.

That's a good idea.
좋은 생각이에요.
jo-eun saeng-ga-gi-ye-yo.

I can't say no.
아니라고 할 수 없어요.
a-ni-ra-go hal su eop-seo-yo.

I'd be happy to.
기쁘게 할게요.
gi-ppeu-ge hal-ge-yo.

With pleasure.
기꺼이요.
gi-kkeo-i-yo.

Refusal. Expressing doubt

No.
아니오.
a-ni-o.

Certainly not.
절대 아니예요.
jeol-dae a-ni-ye-yo.

I don't agree.
동의할 수 없어요.
dong-ui-hal su eop-seo-yo.

I don't think so.
그렇게 생각 안 해요.
geu-reo-ke saeng-gak gan hae-yo.

It's not true.
그렇지 않아요.
geu-reo-chi a-na-yo.

You are wrong.
틀렸어요.
teul-lyeo-seo-yo.

I think you are wrong.
틀리신 거 같아요.
teul-li-sin geo ga-ta-yo.

I'm not sure.
잘 모르겠어요.
jal mo-reu-ge-seo-yo.

It's impossible.
불가능해요.
bul-ga-neung-hae-yo.

Nothing of the kind (sort)!
그럴 리가요!
geu-reol li-ga-yo!

The exact opposite.
정 반대예요.
jeong ban-dae-ye-yo.

I'm against it.
저는 반대예요.
jeo-neun ban-dae-ye-yo.

I don't care.
저는 신경 안 써요.
jeo-neun sin-gyeong an sseo-yo.

I have no idea.
모르겠어요.
mo-reu-ge-seo-yo.

I doubt it.
그건 아닌 것 같아요.
geu-geon a-nin geot ga-ta-yo.

Sorry, I can't.
죄송합니다. 못 해요.
joe-song-ham-ni-da. mot tae-yo.

Sorry, I don't want to.
죄송합니다. 하기 싫어요.
joe-song-ham-ni-da. ha-gi si-reo-yo.

Thank you, but I don't need this.
감사합니다, 하지만 필요 없어요.
gam-sa-ham-ni-da, ha-ji-man pi-ryo eop-seo-yo.

It's getting late.
좀 늦었네요.
jom neu-jeon-ne-yo.

I have to get up early.

일찍 일어나야 해요.
il-jjik gi-reo-na-ya hae-yo.

I don't feel well.

몸이 안 좋아요.
mom-i an jo-a-yo.

Expressing gratitude

Thank you.
감사합니다.
gam-sa-ham-ni-da.

Thank you very much.
대단히 감사합니다.
dae-dan-hi gam-sa-ham-ni-da.

I really appreciate it.
정말로 감사히
생각해요.
jeong-mal-lo gam-sa-hi
saeng-gak-ae-yo.

I'm really grateful to you.
당신에게 정말로
감사해요.
dang-sin-e-ge jeong-mal-lo
gam-sa-hae-yo.

We are really grateful to you.
저희는 당신에게 정말로
감사해요.
jeo-hui-neun dang-sin-e-ge jeong-mal-lo
gam-sa-hae-yo.

Thank you for your time.
시간 내 주셔서
감사합니다.
si-gan nae ju-syeo-seo
gam-sa-ham-ni-da.

Thanks for everything.
전부 다 감사합니다.
jeon-bu da gam-sa-ham-ni-da.

Thank you for ...
…에 대해 감사합니다.
...e dae-hae gam-sa-ham-ni-da.

your help
도움
do-um

a nice time
즐거운 시간
jeul-geo-un si-gan

a wonderful meal
훌륭한 식사
hul-lyung-han sik-sa

a pleasant evening
만족스러운 저녁
man-jok-seu-reo-un jeo-nyeok

a wonderful day
훌륭한 하루
hul-lyung-han ha-ru

an amazing journey
근사한 여행
geun-sa-han nyeo-haeng

Don't mention it.
별 말씀을요.
byeol mal-sseu-meu-ryo.

You are welcome.
천만에요.
cheon-man-e-yo.

Any time.
언제든지요.
eon-je-deun-ji-yo.

My pleasure.

제가 즐거웠어요.
je-ga jeul-geo-wo-seo-yo.

Forget it.

됐어요.
dwae-seo-yo.

Don't worry about it.

걱정하지 마세요.
geok-jeong-ha-ji ma-se-yo.

Congratulations. Best wishes

Congratulations!	축하합니다! chuk-a-ham-ni-da!
Happy birthday!	생일 축하합니다! saeng-il chuk-a-ham-ni-da!
Merry Christmas!	메리 크리스마스! me-ri keu-ri-seu-ma-seu!
Happy New Year!	새해 복 많이 받으세요! sae-hae bok ma-ni ba-deu-se-yo!
Happy Easter!	즐거운 부활절 되세요! jeul-geo-un bu-hwal-jeol doe-se-yo!
Happy Hanukkah!	즐거운 하누카 되세요! jeul-geo-un ha-nu-ka doe-se-yo!
I'd like to propose a toast.	건배해요. geon-bae-hae-yo.
Cheers!	건배! geon-bae!
Let's drink to ...!	… 위하여! ... wi-ha-yeo!
To our success!	성공을 위하여! seong-gong-eul rwi-ha-yeo!
To your success!	성공을 위하여! seong-gong-eul rwi-ha-yeo!
Good luck!	행운을 빌어! haeng-u-neul bi-reo!
Have a nice day!	좋은 하루 되세요! jo-eun ha-ru doe-se-yo!
Have a good holiday!	좋은 휴일 되세요! jo-eun hyu-il doe-se-yo!
Have a safe journey!	안전한 여행 되세요! an-jeon-han nyeo-haeng doe-se-yo!
I hope you get better soon!	빨리 나으세요! ppal-li na-eu-se-yo!

Socializing

Why are you sad?
왜 슬퍼하세요?
wae seul-peo-ha-se-yo?

Smile! Cheer up!
웃으세요! 기운 내세요!
us-eu-se-yo! gi-un nae-se-yo!

Are you free tonight?
오늘 밤에 시간 있으세요?
o-neul bam-e si-gan i-seu-se-yo?

May I offer you a drink?
제가 한 잔 살까요?
je-ga han jan sal-kka-yo?

Would you like to dance?
춤 추실래요?
chum chu-sil-lae-yo?

Let's go to the movies.
영화 보러 갑시다.
yeong-hwa bo-reo gap-si-da.

May I invite you to ...?
…에 초대해도 될까요?
...e cho-dae-hae-do doel-kka-yo?

a restaurant
음식점
eum-sik-jeom

the movies
영화관
yeong-hwa-gwan

the theater
극장
geuk-jang

go for a walk
산책
san-chaek

At what time?
몇 시예요?
myeot si-e-yo?

tonight
오늘밤
o-neul-bam

at six
여섯 시
yeo-seot si

at seven
일곱 시
il-gop si

at eight
여덟 시
yeo-deol si

at nine
아홉 시
a-hop si

Do you like it here?
여기가 마음에 드세요?
yeo-gi-ga ma-eum-e deu-se-yo?

Are you here with someone?
누구랑 같이 왔어요?
nu-gu-rang ga-chi wa-seo-yo?

I'm with my friend.
친구랑 같이 왔어요.
chin-gu-rang ga-chi wa-seo-yo.

I'm with my friends.	친구들이랑 같이 왔어요. chin-gu-deu-ri-rang ga-chi wa-seo-yo.
No, I'm alone.	아니오, 혼자 왔어요. a-ni-o, hon-ja wa-seo-yo.

Do you have a boyfriend?	남자친구 있어? nam-ja-chin-gu i-seo?
I have a boyfriend.	남자친구 있어. nam-ja-chin-gu i-seo.
Do you have a girlfriend?	여자친구 있어? yeo-ja-chin-gu i-seo?
I have a girlfriend.	여자친구 있어. yeo-ja-chin-gu i-seo.

Can I see you again?	다시 만날래? da-si man-nal-lae?
Can I call you?	전화해도 돼? jeon-hwa-hae-do dwae?
Call me. (Give me a call.)	전화해 줘. jeon-hwa-hae jwo.
What's your number?	전화번호가 뭐야? jeon-hwa-beon-ho-ga mwo-ya?
I miss you.	보고싶어. bo-go-si-peo.

You have a beautiful name.	이름이 아름다우시네요. i-reum-i a-reum-da-u-si-ne-yo.
I love you.	사랑해. sa-rang-hae.
Will you marry me?	결혼해 줄래? gyeol-hon-hae jul-lae?
You're kidding!	장난치지 마세요! jang-nan-chi-ji ma-se-yo!
I'm just kidding.	장난이었어요. jang-nan-i-eo-seo-yo.

Are you serious?	진심이세요? jin-sim-i-se-yo?
I'm serious.	진심이예요. jin-sim-i-ye-yo.
Really?!	정말로요?! jeong-mal-lo-yo?!
It's unbelievable!	믿을 수 없어요! mi-deul su eop-seo-yo!
I don't believe you.	당신을 믿지 않아요. dang-si-neul mit-ji a-na-yo.

I can't.	그럴 수 없어요. geu-reol su eop-seo-yo.
I don't know.	모르겠어요. mo-reu-ge-seo-yo.

I don't understand you.	무슨 말인지 모르겠어요.
	mu-seun ma-rin-ji mo-reu-ge-seo-yo.
Please go away.	저리 가세요.
	jeo-ri ga-se-yo.
Leave me alone!	혼자 있고 싶어요!
	hon-ja it-go si-peo-yo!

I can't stand him.	그를 견딜 수 없어요.
	geu-reul gyeon-dil su eop-seo-yo.
You are disgusting!	당신 역겨워요!
	dang-sin nyeok-gyeo-wo-yo!
I'll call the police!	경찰을 부를 거예요!
	gyeong-cha-reul bu-reul geo-ye-yo!

Sharing impressions. Emotions

I like it.	마음에 들어요. ma-eum-e deu-reo-yo.
Very nice.	아주 좋아요. a-ju jo-a-yo.
That's great!	멋져요! meot-jyeo-yo!
It's not bad.	나쁘지 않아요. na-ppeu-ji a-na-yo.

I don't like it.	마음에 들지 않아요. ma-eum-e deul-ji a-na-yo.
It's not good.	좋지 않아요. jo-chi a-na-yo.
It's bad.	나빠요. na-ppa-yo.
It's very bad.	아주 나빠요. a-ju na-ppa-yo.
It's disgusting.	역겨워요. yeok-gyeo-wo-yo.

I'm happy.	저는 행복해요. jeo-neun haeng-bok-ae-yo.
I'm content.	저는 만족해요. jeo-neun man-jok-ae-yo.
I'm in love.	저는 사랑에 빠졌어요. jeo-neun sa-rang-e ppa-jyeo-seo-yo.
I'm calm.	저는 침착해요. jeo-neun chim-chak-ae-yo.
I'm bored.	저는 지루해요. jeo-neun ji-ru-hae-yo.

I'm tired.	저는 지쳤어요. jeo-neun ji-chyeo-seo-yo.
I'm sad.	저는 슬퍼요. jeo-neun seul-peo-yo.
I'm frightened.	저는 무서워요. jeo-neun mu-seo-wo-yo.

I'm angry.	저는 화났어요. jeo-neun hwa-na-seo-yo.
I'm worried.	저는 걱정이 돼요. jeo-neun geok-jeong-i dwae-yo.
I'm nervous.	저는 긴장이 돼요. jeo-neun gin-jang-i dwae-yo.

I'm jealous. (envious)

저는 부러워요.
jeo-neun bu-reo-wo-yo.

I'm surprised.

놀랐어요.
nol-la-seo-yo.

I'm perplexed.

당황했어요.
dang-hwang-hae-seo-yo.

Problems. Accidents

I've got a problem.
문제가 있어요.
mun-je-ga i-seo-yo.

We've got a problem.
우리는 문제가 있어요.
u-ri-neun mun-je-ga i-seo-yo.

I'm lost.
길을 잃었어요.
gi-reul ri-reo-seo-yo.

I missed the last bus (train).
마지막 버스 (기차)를
놓쳤어요.
ma-ji-mak beo-seu (gi-cha)reul
lo-chyeo-seo-yo.

I don't have any money left.
돈이 다 떨어졌어요.
don-i da tteo-reo-jyeo-seo-yo.

I've lost my ...
··· 잃어버렸어요.
... i-reo-beo-ryeo-seo-yo.

Someone stole my ...
제 ··· 누가 훔쳐갔어요.
je ... nu-ga hum-chyeo-ga-seo-yo.

passport
여권
yeo-gwon

wallet
지갑
ji-gap

papers
서류
seo-ryu

ticket
표
pyo

money
돈
don

handbag
핸드백
haen-deu-baek

camera
카메라
ka-me-ra

laptop
노트북
no-teu-buk

tablet computer
타블렛피씨
ta-beul-let-pi-ssi

mobile phone
핸드폰
haen-deu-pon

Help me!
도와주세요!
do-wa-ju-se-yo!

What's happened?
무슨 일이 있었어요?
mu-seun i-ri i-seo-seo-yo?

fire
화재
hwa-jae

shooting	총격 chong-gyeok
murder	살인 sa-rin
explosion	폭발 pok-bal
fight	폭행 pok-aeng

Call the police!	경찰을 불러 주세요! gyeong-cha-reul bul-leo ju-se-yo!
Please hurry up!	제발 서둘러요! je-bal seo-dul-leo-yo!
I'm looking for the police station.	경찰서를 찾고 있어요. gyeong-chal-seo-reul chat-go i-seo-yo.
I need to make a call.	전화를 걸어야 해요. jeon-hwa-reul geo-reo-ya hae-yo.
May I use your phone?	전화를 빌려주실 수 있어요? jeon-hwa-reul bil-lyeo-ju-sil su i-seo-yo?

I've been ...	저는 … 당했어요. jeo-neun ... dang-hae-seo-yo.
mugged	강도 gang-do
robbed	도둑질 do-duk-jil
raped	강간 gang-gan
attacked (beaten up)	폭행 pok-aeng

Are you all right?	괜찮으세요? gwaen-cha-neu-se-yo?
Did you see who it was?	누구였는지 보셨어요? nu-gu-yeon-neun-ji bo-syeo-seo-yo?
Would you be able to recognize the person?	그 사람을 알아볼 수 있겠어요? geu sa-ra-meul ra-ra-bol su it-ge-seo-yo?
Are you sure?	확실해요? hwak-sil-hae-yo?

Please calm down.	제발 진정해요. je-bal jin-jeong-hae-yo.
Take it easy!	마음을 가라앉히세요! ma-eu-meul ga-ra-an-chi-se-yo!
Don't worry!	걱정하지 마세요! geok-jeong-ha-ji ma-se-yo!
Everything will be fine.	다 잘 될 거예요. da jal doel geo-ye-yo.
Everything's all right.	다 괜찮아요. da gwaen-cha-na-yo.

Come here, please.

이 쪽으로 오세요.
i jjo-geu-ro o-se-yo.

I have some questions for you.

질문이 있습니다.
jil-mun-i it-seum-ni-da.

Wait a moment, please.

잠시 기다려 주세요.
jam-si gi-da-ryeo ju-se-yo.

Do you have any I.D.?

신분증 있습니까?
sin-bun-jeung it-seum-ni-kka?

Thanks. You can leave now.

감사합니다. 이제 가져도
됩니다.
gam-sa-ham-ni-da. i-je ga-syeo-do
doem-ni-da.

Hands behind your head!

손 머리 위로 들어!
son meo-ri wi-ro deu-reo!

You're under arrest!

체포한다!
che-po-han-da!

Health problems

Please help me.	도와주세요. do-wa-ju-se-yo.
I don't feel well.	몸이 안 좋아요. mom-i an jo-a-yo.
My husband doesn't feel well.	제 남편이 몸이 안 좋아요. je nam-pyeon-i mom-i an jo-a-yo.
My son ...	제 아들이 ··· je a-deu-ri ...
My father ...	제 아버지가 ··· je a-beo-ji-ga ...
My wife doesn't feel well.	제 아내가 몸이 안 좋아요. je a-nae-ga mom-i an jo-a-yo.
My daughter ...	제 딸이 ··· je tta-ri ...
My mother ...	제 어머니가 ··· je eo-meo-ni-ga ...
I've got a ...	···이 있어요. ...i i-seo-yo.
headache	두통 du-tong
sore throat	인후통 in-hu-tong
stomach ache	복통 bok-tong
toothache	치통 chi-tong
I feel dizzy.	어지러워요. eo-ji-reo-wo-yo.
He has a fever.	그는 열이 있어요. geu-neun nyeo-ri i-seo-yo.
She has a fever.	그녀는 열이 있어요. geu-nyeo-neun nyeo-ri i-seo-yo.
I can't breathe.	숨을 못 쉬겠어요. su-meul mot swi-ge-seo-yo.
I'm short of breath.	숨이 차요. sum-i cha-yo.
I am asthmatic.	저는 천식이 있어요. jeo-neun cheon-si-gi i-seo-yo.
I am diabetic.	저는 당뇨가 있어요. jeo-neun dang-nyo-ga i-seo-yo.

I can't sleep.	저는 잠을 못 자요. jeo-neun ja-meul mot ja-yo.
food poisoning	식중독 sik-jung-dok

It hurts here.	여기가 아파요. yeo-gi-ga a-pa-yo.
Help me!	도와주세요! do-wa-ju-se-yo!
I am here!	여기 있어요! yeo-gi i-seo-yo!
We are here!	우리 여기 있어요! u-ri yeo-gi i-seo-yo!
Get me out of here!	꺼내주세요! kkeo-nae-ju-se-yo!
I need a doctor.	의사가 필요해요. ui-sa-ga pi-ryo-hae-yo.
I can't move.	못 움직이겠어요. mot um-ji-gi-ge-seo-yo.
I can't move my legs.	다리를 못 움직이겠어요. da-ri-reul mot um-ji-gi-ge-seo-yo.

I have a wound.	다쳤어요. da-chyeo-seo-yo.
Is it serious?	심각한가요? sim-gak-an-ga-yo?
My documents are in my pocket.	주머니에 제 서류가 있어요. ju-meo-ni-e je seo-ryu-ga i-seo-yo.
Calm down!	진정해요! jin-jeong-hae-yo!
May I use your phone?	전화를 빌려주실 수 있어요? jeon-hwa-reul bil-lyeo-ju-sil su i-seo-yo?

Call an ambulance!	구급차를 불러 주세요! gu-geup-cha-reul bul-leo ju-se-yo!
It's urgent!	급해요! geu-pae-yo!
It's an emergency!	긴급 상황이에요! gin-geup sang-hwang-i-e-yo!
Please hurry up!	제발 서둘러요! je-bal seo-dul-leo-yo!
Would you please call a doctor?	의사를 불러주시겠어요? ui-sa-reul bul-leo-ju-si-ge-seo-yo?
Where is the hospital?	병원은 어디 있어요? byeong-wo-neun eo-di i-seo-yo?

How are you feeling?	기분이 어떠세요? gi-bun-i eo-tteo-se-yo?
Are you all right?	괜찮으세요? gwaen-cha-neu-se-yo?
What's happened?	무슨 일이 있었어요? mu-seun i-ri i-seo-seo-yo?

I feel better now.

이제 나아졌어요.
i-je na-a-jyeo-seo-yo.

It's OK.

괜찮아요.
gwaen-cha-na-yo.

It's all right.

괜찮아요.
gwaen-cha-na-yo.

At the pharmacy

pharmacy (drugstore)	약국 yak-guk
24-hour pharmacy	24시간 약국 i-sip-sa-si-gan nyak-guk
Where is the closest pharmacy?	가장 가까운 약국이 어디예요? ga-jang ga-kka-un nyak-gu-gi eo-di-ye-yo?

Is it open now?	지금 열었어요? ji-geum myeo-reo-seo-yo?
At what time does it open?	몇 시에 열어요? myeot si-e yeo-reo-yo?
At what time does it close?	몇 시에 닫아요? myeot si-e da-da-yo?

Is it far?	멀어요? meo-reo-yo?
Can I get there on foot?	걸어갈 수 있어요? geo-reo-gal su i-seo-yo?
Can you show me on the map?	지도에서 보여주실 수 있어요? ji-do-e-seo bo-yeo-ju-sil su i-seo-yo?

Please give me something for ...	···에 듣는 약 주세요. ...e deun-neun nyak ju-se-yo.
a headache	두통 du-tong
a cough	기침 gi-chim
a cold	감기 gam-gi
the flu	독감 dok-gam

a fever	열 yeol
a stomach ache	복통 bok-tong
nausea	구토 gu-to
diarrhea	설사 seol-sa
constipation	변비 byeon-bi

pain in the back

등 통증
deung tong-jeung

chest pain

가슴 통증
ga-seum tong-jeung

side stitch

옆구리 당김
yeop-gu-ri dang-gim

abdominal pain

배 통증
bae tong-jeung

pill

알약
a-ryak

ointment, cream

연고
yeon-go

syrup

물약
mul-lyak

spray

스프레이
seu-peu-re-i

drops

안약
a-nyak

You need to go to the hospital.

병원에 가셔야 해요.
byeong-won-e ga-syeo-ya hae-yo.

health insurance

건강보험
geon-gang-bo-heom

prescription

처방전
cheo-bang-jeon

insect repellant

방충제
bang-chung-je

Band Aid

밴드에이드
baen-deu-e-i-deu

The bare minimum

Excuse me, ...
실례합니다, ···
sil-lye-ham-ni-da, ...

Hello.
안녕하세요.
an-nyeong-ha-se-yo.

Thank you.
감사합니다.
gam-sa-ham-ni-da.

Good bye.
안녕히 계세요.
an-nyeong-hi gye-se-yo.

Yes.
네.
ne.

No.
아니오.
a-ni-o.

I don't know.
모르겠어요.
mo-reu-ge-seo-yo.

Where? | Where to? | When?
어디예요? | 어디까지 가세요? |
언제요?
eo-di-ye-yo? | eo-di-kka-ji ga-se-yo? |
eon-je-yo?

I need ...
··· 필요해요.
... pi-ryo-hae-yo.

I want ...
··· 싶어요.
... si-peo-yo.

Do you have ...?
··· 있으세요?
... i-seu-se-yo?

Is there a ... here?
여기 ··· 있어요?
yeo-gi ... i-seo-yo?

May I ...?
···해도 되나요?
... hae-do doe-na-yo?

..., please (polite request)
···, 부탁합니다.
..., bu-tak-am-ni-da.

I'm looking for ...
··· 찾고 있어요.
... chat-go i-seo-yo.

restroom
화장실
hwa-jang-sil

ATM
현금인출기
hyeon-geum-in-chul-gi

pharmacy (drugstore)
약국
yak-guk

hospital
병원
byeong-won

police station
경찰서
gyeong-chal-seo

subway	지하철 ji-ha-cheol
taxi	택시 taek-si
train station	기차역 gi-cha-yeok

My name is ...	제 이름은 … 입니다. je i-reu-meun ... im-ni-da.
What's your name?	성함이 어떻게 되세요? seong-ham-i eo-tteo-ke doe-se-yo?
Could you please help me?	도와주세요. do-wa-ju-se-yo.
I've got a problem.	문제가 있어요. mun-je-ga i-seo-yo.
I don't feel well.	몸이 안 좋아요. mom-i an jo-a-yo.
Call an ambulance!	구급차를 불러 주세요! gu-geup-cha-reul bul-leo ju-se-yo!
May I make a call?	전화를 써도 되나요? jeon-hwa-reul sseo-do doe-na-yo?

I'm sorry.	죄송합니다. joe-song-ham-ni-da.
You're welcome.	천만에요. cheon-man-e-yo.

I, me	저 jeo
you (inform.)	너 neo
he	그 geu
she	그녀 geu-nyeo
they (masc.)	그들 geu-deul
they (fem.)	그들 geu-deul
we	우리 u-ri
you (pl)	너희 neo-hui
you (sg, form.)	당신 dang-sin

ENTRANCE	입구 ip-gu
EXIT	출구 chul-gu
OUT OF ORDER	고장 go-jang

CLOSED

닫힘
da-chim

OPEN

열림
yeol-lim

FOR WOMEN

여성용
yeo-seong-yong

FOR MEN

남성용
nam-seong-yong

CONCISE DICTIONARY

This section contains more than 1,500 useful words arranged alphabetically. The dictionary includes a lot of gastronomic terms and will be helpful when ordering food at a restaurant or buying groceries

T&P Books Publishing

DICTIONARY CONTENTS

T&P Books Publishing

T&P Books Publishing

time	시간	si-gan
hour	시	si
half an hour	반시간	ban-si-gan
minute	분	bun
second	초	cho
today (adv)	오늘	o-neul
tomorrow (adv)	내일	nae-il
yesterday (adv)	어제	eo-je
Monday	월요일	wo-ryo-il
Tuesday	화요일	hwa-yo-il
Wednesday	수요일	su-yo-il
Thursday	목요일	mo-gyo-il
Friday	금요일	geu-myo-il
Saturday	토요일	to-yo-il
Sunday	일요일	i-ryo-il
day	낮	nat
working day	근무일	geun-mu-il
public holiday	공휴일	gong-hyu-il
weekend	주말	ju-mal
week	주	ju
last week (adv)	지난 주에	ji-nan ju-e
next week (adv)	다음 주에	da-eum ju-e
sunrise	일출	il-chul
sunset	저녁 노을	jeo-nyeok no-eul
in the morning	아침에	a-chim-e
in the afternoon	오후에	o-hu-e
in the evening	저녁에	jeo-nyeo-ge
tonight (this evening)	오늘 저녁에	o-neul jeo-nyeo-ge
at night	밤에	bam-e
midnight	자정	ja-jeong
January	일월	i-rwol
February	이월	i-wol
March	삼월	sam-wol
April	사월	sa-wol
May	오월	o-wol
June	유월	yu-wol

July	칠월	chi-rwol
August	팔월	pa-rwol
September	구월	gu-wol
October	시월	si-wol
November	십일월	si-bi-rwol
December	십이월	si-bi-wol
in spring	봄에	bom-e
in summer	여름에	yeo-reum-e
in fall	가을에	ga-eu-re
in winter	겨울에	gyeo-u-re
month	월, 달	wol, dal
season (summer, etc.)	계절	gye-jeol
year	년	nyeon
century	세기	se-gi

2. Numbers. Numerals

digit, figure	숫자	sut-ja
number	숫자	sut-ja
minus sign	마이너스	ma-i-neo-seu
plus sign	플러스	peul-leo-seu
sum, total	총합	chong-hap
first (adj)	첫 번째의	cheot beon-jjae-ui
second (adj)	두 번째의	du beon-jjae-ui
third (adj)	세 번째의	se beon-jjae-ui
0 zero	영	yeong
1 one	일	il
2 two	이	i
3 three	삼	sam
4 four	사	sa
5 five	오	o
6 six	육	yuk
7 seven	칠	chil
8 eight	팔	pal
9 nine	구	gu
10 ten	십	sip
11 eleven	십일	si-bil
12 twelve	십이	si-bi
13 thirteen	십삼	sip-sam
14 fourteen	십사	sip-sa
15 fifteen	십오	si-bo
16 sixteen	십육	si-byuk
17 seventeen	십칠	sip-chil

18 eighteen	십팔	sip-pal
19 nineteen	십구	sip-gu
20 twenty	이십	i-sip
30 thirty	삼십	sam-sip
40 forty	사십	sa-sip
50 fifty	오십	o-sip
60 sixty	육십	yuk-sip
70 seventy	칠십	chil-sip
80 eighty	팔십	pal-sip
90 ninety	구십	gu-sip
100 one hundred	백	baek
200 two hundred	이백	i-baek
300 three hundred	삼백	sam-baek
400 four hundred	사백	sa-baek
500 five hundred	오백	o-baek
600 six hundred	육백	yuk-baek
700 seven hundred	칠백	chil-baek
800 eight hundred	팔백	pal-baek
900 nine hundred	구백	gu-baek
1000 one thousand	천	cheon
10000 ten thousand	만	man
one hundred thousand	십만	sim-man
million	백만	baeng-man
billion	십억	si-beok

3. Humans. Family

man (adult male)	남자	nam-ja
young man	젊은 분	jeol-meun bun
teenager	청소년	cheong-so-nyeon
woman	여자	yeo-ja
girl (young woman)	소녀, 아가씨	so-nyeo, a-ga-ssi
age	나이	na-i
adult (adj)	어른	eo-reun
middle-aged (adj)	중년의	jung-nyeo-nui
elderly (adj)	나이 든	na-i deun
old (adj)	늙은	neul-geun
old man	노인	no-in
old woman	노인	no-in
retirement	은퇴	eun-toe
to retire (from job)	은퇴하다	eun-toe-ha-da
retiree	은퇴자	eun-toe-ja

mother	어머니	eo-meo-ni
father	아버지	a-beo-ji
son	아들	a-deul
daughter	딸	ttal
brother	형제	hyeong-je
sister	자매	ja-mae
parents	부모	bu-mo
child	아이, 아동	a-i, a-dong
children	아이들	a-i-deul
stepmother	계모	gye-mo
stepfather	계부	gye-bu
grandmother	할머니	hal-meo-ni
grandfather	할아버지	ha-ra-beo-ji
grandson	손자	son-ja
granddaughter	손녀	son-nyeo
grandchildren	손자들	son-ja-deul
uncle	삼촌	sam-chon
nephew	조카	jo-ka
niece	조카딸	jo-ka-ttal
wife	아내	a-nae
husband	남편	nam-pyeon
married (masc.)	결혼한	gyeol-hon-han
married (fem.)	결혼한	gyeol-hon-han
widow	과부	gwa-bu
widower	홀아비	ho-ra-bi
name (first name)	이름	i-reum
surname (last name)	성	seong
relative	친척	chin-cheok
friend (masc.)	친구	chin-gu
friendship	우정	u-jeong
partner	파트너	pa-teu-neo
superior (n)	윗사람	wit-sa-ram
colleague	동료	dong-nyo
neighbors	이웃들	i-ut-deul

4. Human body

organism (body)	생체	saeng-che
body	몸	mom
heart	심장	sim-jang
blood	피	pi
brain	두뇌	du-noe
nerve	신경	sin-gyeong

bone	뼈	ppyeo
skeleton	뼈대	ppyeo-dae
spine (backbone)	등뼈	deung-ppyeo
rib	늑골	neuk-gol
skull	두개골	du-gae-gol
muscle	근육	geu-nyuk
lungs	폐	pye
skin	피부	pi-bu
head	머리	meo-ri
face	얼굴	eol-gul
nose	코	ko
forehead	이마	i-ma
cheek	뺨, 볼	ppyam, bol
mouth	입	ip
tongue	혀	hyeo
tooth	이	i
lips	입술	ip-sul
chin	턱	teok
ear	귀	gwi
neck	목	mok
throat	목구멍	mok-gu-meong
eye	눈	nun
pupil	눈동자	nun-dong-ja
eyebrow	눈썹	nun-sseop
eyelash	속눈썹	song-nun-sseop
hair	머리털, 헤어	meo-ri-teol, he-eo
hairstyle	머리 스타일	meo-ri seu-ta-il
mustache	콧수염	kot-su-yeom
beard	턱수염	teok-su-yeom
to have (a beard, etc.)	기르다	gi-reu-da
bald (adj)	대머리인	dae-meo-ri-in
hand	손	son
arm	팔	pal
finger	손가락	son-ga-rak
nail	손톱	son-top
palm	손바닥	son-ba-dak
shoulder	어깨	eo-kkae
leg	다리	da-ri
foot	발	bal
knee	무릎	mu-reup
heel	발뒤꿈치	bal-dwi-kkum-chi
back	등	deung
waist	허리	heo-ri

beauty mark	점	jeom
birthmark (café au lait spot)	모반	mo-ban

5. Medicine. Diseases. Drugs

health	건강	geon-gang
well (not sick)	건강한	geon-gang-han
sickness	병	byeong
to be sick	눕다	nup-da
ill, sick (adj)	아픈	a-peun
cold (illness)	감기	gam-gi
to catch a cold	감기에 걸리다	gam-gi-e geol-li-da
tonsillitis	편도염	pyeon-do-yeom
pneumonia	폐렴	pye-ryeom
flu, influenza	독감	dok-gam
runny nose (coryza)	비염	bi-yeom
cough	기침	gi-chim
to cough (vi)	기침을 하다	gi-chi-meul ha-da
to sneeze (vi)	재채기하다	jae-chae-gi-ha-da
stroke	뇌졸중	noe-jol-jung
heart attack	심장마비	sim-jang-ma-bi
allergy	알레르기	al-le-reu-gi
asthma	천식	cheon-sik
diabetes	당뇨병	dang-nyo-byeong
tumor	종양	jong-yang
cancer	암	am
alcoholism	알코올 중독	al-ko-ol jung-dok
AIDS	에이즈	e-i-jeu
fever	열병	yeol-byeong
seasickness	뱃멀미	baen-meol-mi
bruise (hématome)	멍	meong
bump (lump)	혹	hok
to limp (vi)	절다	jeol-da
dislocation	탈구	tal-gu
to dislocate (vt)	탈구하다	tal-gu-ha-da
fracture	골절	gol-jeol
burn (injury)	화상	hwa-sang
injury	부상	bu-sang
pain, ache	통증	tong-jeung
toothache	치통, 이앓이	chi-tong, i-a-ri
to sweat (perspire)	땀이 나다	ttam-i na-da
deaf (adj)	귀가 먼	gwi-ga meon

mute (adj)	병어리인	beong-eo-ri-in
immunity	면역성	myeo-nyeok-seong
virus	바이러스	ba-i-reo-seu
microbe	미생물	mi-saeng-mul
bacterium	세균	se-gyun
infection	감염	gam-nyeom
hospital	병원	byeong-won
cure	치료	chi-ryo
to vaccinate (vt)	접종하다	jeop-jong-ha-da
to be in a coma	혼수 상태에 있다	hon-su sang-tae-e it-da
intensive care	집중 치료	jip-jung chi-ryo
symptom	증상	jeung-sang
pulse	맥박	maek-bak

6. Feelings. Emotions. Conversation

I, me	나, 저	na
you	너	neo
he	그, 그분	geu, geu-bun
she	그녀	geu-nyeo
it	그것	geu-geot
we	우리	u-ri
you (to a group)	너희	neo-hui
you (polite, sing.)	당신	dang-sin
they	그들	geu-deul
Hello! (fam.)	안녕!	an-nyeong!
Hello! (form.)	안녕하세요!	an-nyeong-ha-se-yo!
Good morning!	안녕하세요!	an-nyeong-ha-se-yo!
Good afternoon!	안녕하세요!	an-nyeong-ha-se-yo!
Good evening!	안녕하세요!	an-nyeong-ha-se-yo!
to say hello	인사하다	in-sa-ha-da
to greet (vt)	인사하다	in-sa-ha-da
How are you?	잘 지내세요?	jal ji-nae-se-yo?
Bye-Bye! Goodbye!	안녕히 가세요!	an-nyeong-hi ga-se-yo!
Thank you!	감사합니다!	gam-sa-ham-ni-da!
feelings	감정	gam-jeong
to be hungry	배가 고프다	bae-ga go-peu-da
to be thirsty	목마르다	mong-ma-reu-da
tired (adj)	피곤한	pi-gon-han
to be worried	걱정하다	geok-jeong-ha-da
to be nervous	긴장하다	gin-jang-ha-da
hope	희망	hui-mang
to hope (vi, vt)	희망하다	hui-mang-ha-da
character	성격	seong-gyeok

modest (adj)	겸손한	gyeom-son-han
lazy (adj)	게으른	ge-eu-reun
generous (adj)	관대한	gwan-dae-han
talented (adj)	재능이 있는	jae-neung-i in-neun

honest (adj)	정직한	jeong-jik-an
serious (adj)	진지한	jin-ji-han
shy, timid (adj)	소심한	so-sim-han
sincere (adj)	성실한	seong-sil-han
coward	비겁한 자, 겁쟁이	bi-geo-pan ja, geop-jaeng-i

to sleep (vi)	잠을 자다	ja-meul ja-da
dream	꿈	kkum
bed	침대	chim-dae
pillow	베개	be-gae

insomnia	불면증	bul-myeon-jeung
to go to bed	잠자리에 들다	jam-ja-ri-e deul-da
nightmare	악몽	ang-mong
alarm clock	알람 시계	al-lam si-gye

smile	미소	mi-so
to smile (vi)	미소를 짓다	mi-so-reul jit-da
to laugh (vi)	웃다	ut-da

quarrel	싸움	ssa-um
insult	모욕	mo-yok
resentment	분노	bun-no
angry (mad)	화가 난	hwa-ga nan

7. Clothing. Personal accessories

clothes	옷	ot
coat (overcoat)	코트	ko-teu
fur coat	모피 외투	mo-pi oe-tu
jacket (e.g., leather ~)	재킷	jae-kit
raincoat (trenchcoat, etc.)	트렌치코트	teu-ren-chi-ko-teu

shirt (button shirt)	셔츠	syeo-cheu
pants	바지	ba-ji
suit jacket	재킷	jae-kit
suit	양복	yang-bok

dress (frock)	드레스	deu-re-seu
skirt	치마	chi-ma
T-shirt	티셔츠	ti-syeo-cheu
bathrobe	목욕가운	mo-gyok-ga-un
pajamas	파자마	pa-ja-ma
workwear	작업복	ja-geop-bok
underwear	속옷	so-got

socks	양말	yang-mal
bra	브라	beu-ra
pantyhose	팬티 스타킹	paen-ti seu-ta-king
stockings (thigh highs)	밴드 스타킹	baen-deu seu-ta-king
bathing suit	수영복	su-yeong-bok

hat	모자	mo-ja
footwear	신발	sin-bal
boots (e.g., cowboy ~)	부츠	bu-cheu
heel	굽	gup
shoestring	끈	kkeun
shoe polish	구두약	gu-du-yak

cotton (n)	면	myeon
wool (n)	모직, 울	mo-jik, ul
fur (n)	모피	mo-pi

gloves	장갑	jang-gap
mittens	벙어리장갑	beong-eo-ri-jang-gap
scarf (muffler)	목도리	mok-do-ri
glasses (eyeglasses)	안경	an-gyeong
umbrella	우산	u-san

tie (necktie)	넥타이	nek-ta-i
handkerchief	손수건	son-su-geon
comb	빗	bit
hairbrush	빗, 솔빗	bit, sol-bit

buckle	버클	beo-keul
belt	벨트	bel-teu
purse	핸드백	haen-deu-baek

collar	옷깃	ot-git
pocket	주머니, 포켓	ju-meo-ni, po-ket
sleeve	소매	so-mae
fly (on trousers)	바지 지퍼	ba-ji ji-peo

zipper (fastener)	지퍼	ji-peo
button	단추	dan-chu
to get dirty (vi)	더러워지다	deo-reo-wo-ji-da
stain (mark, spot)	얼룩	eol-luk

8. City. Urban institutions

store	가게, 상점	ga-ge, sang-jeom
shopping mall	쇼핑몰	syo-ping-mol
supermarket	슈퍼마켓	syu-peo-ma-ket
shoe store	신발 가게	sin-bal ga-ge
bookstore	서점	seo-jeom
drugstore, pharmacy	약국	yak-guk

bakery	빵집	ppang-jip
pastry shop	제과점	je-gwa-jeom
grocery store	식료품점	sing-nyo-pum-jeom
butcher shop	정육점	jeong-yuk-jeom
produce store	야채 가게	ya-chae ga-ge
market	시장	si-jang
hair salon	미장원	mi-jang-won
post office	우체국	u-che-guk
dry cleaners	드라이 클리닝	deu-ra-i keul-li-ning
circus	서커스	seo-keo-seu
zoo	동물원	dong-mu-rwon
theater	극장	geuk-jang
movie theater	영화관	yeong-hwa-gwan
museum	박물관	bang-mul-gwan
library	도서관	do-seo-gwan
mosque	모스크	mo-seu-keu
synagogue	유대교 회당	yu-dae-gyo hoe-dang
cathedral	대성당	dae-seong-dang
temple	사원, 신전	sa-won, sin-jeon
church	교회	gyo-hoe
college	단과대학	dan-gwa-dae-hak
university	대학교	dae-hak-gyo
school	학교	hak-gyo
hotel	호텔	ho-tel
bank	은행	eun-haeng
embassy	대사관	dae-sa-gwan
travel agency	여행사	yeo-haeng-sa
subway	지하철	ji-ha-cheol
hospital	병원	byeong-won
gas station	주유소	ju-yu-so
parking lot	주차장	ju-cha-jang
ENTRANCE	입구	ip-gu
EXIT	출구	chul-gu
PUSH	미세요	mi-se-yo
PULL	당기세요	dang-gi-se-yo
OPEN	열림	yeol-lim
CLOSED	닫힘	da-chim
monument	기념비	gi-nyeom-bi
fortress	요새	yo-sae
palace	궁전	gung-jeon
medieval (adj)	중세의	jung-se-ui
ancient (adj)	고대의	go-dae-ui
national (adj)	국가의	guk-ga-ui
famous (monument, etc.)	유명한	yu-myeong-han

9. Money. Finances

money	돈	don
coin	동전	dong-jeon
dollar	달러	dal-leo
euro	유로	yu-ro
ATM	현금 자동 지급기	hyeon-geum ja-dong ji-geup-gi
currency exchange	환전소	hwan-jeon-so
exchange rate	환율	hwa-nyul
cash	현금	hyeon-geum
How much?	얼마?	eol-ma?
to pay (vi, vt)	지불하다	ji-bul-ha-da
payment	지불	ji-bul
change (give the ~)	거스름돈	geo-seu-reum-don
price	가격	ga-gyeok
discount	할인	ha-rin
cheap (adj)	싼	ssan
expensive (adj)	비싼	bi-ssan
bank	은행	eun-haeng
account	계좌	gye-jwa
credit card	신용 카드	si-nyong ka-deu
check	수표	su-pyo
to write a check	수표를 끊다	su-pyo-reul kkeun-ta
checkbook	수표책	su-pyo-chaek
debt	빚	bit
debtor	채무자	chae-mu-ja
to lend (money)	빌려주다	bil-lyeo-ju-da
to borrow (vi, vt)	빌리다	bil-li-da
to rent (~ a tuxedo)	빌리다	bil-li-da
on credit (adv)	신용으로	si-nyong-eu-ro
wallet	지갑	ji-gap
safe	금고	geum-go
inheritance	유산	yu-san
fortune (wealth)	재산, 큰돈	jae-san, keun-don
tax	세금	se-geum
fine	벌금	beol-geum
to fine (vt)	벌금을 부과하다	beol-geu-meul bu-gwa-ha-da
wholesale (adj)	도매의	do-mae-ui
retail (adj)	소매의	so-mae-ui
to insure (vt)	보험에 들다	bo-heom-e deul-da
insurance	보험	bo-heom

capital	자본	ja-bon
turnover	총매출액	chong-mae-chu-raek
stock (share)	주식	ju-sik
profit	수익, 이익	su-ik, i-ik
profitable (adj)	수익성이 있는	su-ik-seong-i in-neun
crisis	위기	wi-gi
bankruptcy	파산	pa-san
to go bankrupt	파산하다	pa-san-ha-da
accountant	회계사	hoe-gye-sa
salary	급여, 월급	geu-byeo, wol-geup
bonus (money)	보너스	bo-neo-seu

10. Transportation

bus	버스	beo-seu
streetcar	전차	jeon-cha
trolley bus	트롤리 버스	teu-rol-li beo-seu
to go by ...	… 타고 가다	… ta-go ga-da
to get on (~ the bus)	타다	ta-da
to get off ...	… 에서 내리다	… e-seo nae-ri-da
stop (e.g., bus ~)	정류장	jeong-nyu-jang
terminus	종점	jong-jeom
schedule	시간표	si-gan-pyo
ticket	표	pyo
to be late (for ...)	… 시간에 늦다	… si-gan-e neut-da
taxi, cab	택시	taek-si
by taxi	택시로	taek-si-ro
taxi stand	택시 정류장	taek-si jeong-nyu-jang
traffic	교통	gyo-tong
rush hour	러시 아워	reo-si a-wo
to park (vi)	주차하다	ju-cha-ha-da
subway	지하철	ji-ha-cheol
station	역	yeok
train	기차	gi-cha
train station	기차역	gi-cha-yeok
rails	레일	re-il
compartment	침대차	chim-dae-cha
berth	침대	chim-dae
airplane	비행기	bi-haeng-gi
air ticket	비행기표	bi-haeng-gi-pyo
airline	항공사	hang-gong-sa
airport	공항	gong-hang

flight (act of flying)	비행	bi-haeng
luggage	짐, 수하물	jim, su-ha-mul
luggage cart	수하물 카트	su-ha-mul ka-teu
ship	배	bae
cruise ship	크루즈선	keu-ru-jeu-seon
yacht	요트	yo-teu
boat (flat-bottomed ~)	보트	bo-teu
captain	선장	seon-jang
cabin	선실	seon-sil
port (harbor)	항구	hang-gu
bicycle	자전거	ja-jeon-geo
scooter	스쿠터	seu-ku-teo
motorcycle, bike	오토바이	o-to-ba-i
pedal	페달	pe-dal
pump	펌프	peom-peu
wheel	바퀴	ba-kwi
automobile, car	자동차	ja-dong-cha
ambulance	응급차	eung-geup-cha
truck	트럭	teu-reok
used (adj)	중고의	jung-go-ui
car crash	사고	sa-go
repair	수리	su-ri

11. Food. Part 1

meat	고기	go-gi
chicken	닭고기	dak-go-gi
duck	오리고기	o-ri-go-gi
pork	돼지고기	dwae-ji-go-gi
veal	송아지 고기	song-a-ji go-gi
lamb	양고기	yang-go-gi
beef	소고기	so-go-gi
sausage (bologna, pepperoni, etc.)	소시지	so-si-ji
egg	계란	gye-ran
fish	생선	saeng-seon
cheese	치즈	chi-jeu
sugar	설탕	seol-tang
salt	소금	so-geum
rice	쌀	ssal
pasta (macaroni)	파스타	pa-seu-ta
butter	버터	beo-teo
vegetable oil	식물유	sing-mu-ryu

bread	빵	ppang
chocolate (n)	초콜릿	cho-kol-lit
wine	와인	wa-in
coffee	커피	keo-pi
milk	우유	u-yu
juice	주스	ju-seu
beer	맥주	maek-ju
tea	차	cha
tomato	토마토	to-ma-to
cucumber	오이	o-i
carrot	당근	dang-geun
potato	감자	gam-ja
onion	양파	yang-pa
garlic	마늘	ma-neul
cabbage	양배추	yang-bae-chu
beetroot	비트	bi-teu
eggplant	가지	ga-ji
dill	딜	dil
lettuce	양상추	yang-sang-chu
corn (maize)	옥수수	ok-su-su
fruit	과일	gwa-il
apple	사과	sa-gwa
pear	배	bae
lemon	레몬	re-mon
orange	오렌지	o-ren-ji
strawberry (garden ~)	딸기	ttal-gi
plum	자두	ja-du
raspberry	라즈베리	ra-jeu-be-ri
pineapple	파인애플	pa-in-ae-peul
banana	바나나	ba-na-na
watermelon	수박	su-bak
grape	포도	po-do
melon	멜론	mel-lon

12. Food. Part 2

cuisine	요리	yo-ri
recipe	요리법	yo-ri-beop
food	음식	eum-sik
to have breakfast	아침을 먹다	a-chi-meul meok-da
to have lunch	점심을 먹다	jeom-si-meul meok-da
to have dinner	저녁을 먹다	jeo-nyeo-geul meok-da
taste, flavor	맛	mat
tasty (adj)	맛있는	man-nin-neun

cold (adj)	차가운	cha-ga-un
hot (adj)	뜨거운	tteu-geo-un
sweet (sugary)	단	dan
salty (adj)	짠	jjan

sandwich (bread)	샌드위치	saen-deu-wi-chi
side dish	사이드 메뉴	sa-i-deu me-nyu
filling (for cake, pie)	속	sok
sauce	소스	so-seu
piece (of cake, pie)	조각	jo-gak

diet	다이어트	da-i-eo-teu
vitamin	비타민	bi-ta-min
calorie	칼로리	kal-lo-ri
vegetarian (n)	채식주의자	chae-sik-ju-ui-ja

restaurant	레스토랑	re-seu-to-rang
coffee house	커피숍	keo-pi-syop
appetite	식욕	si-gyok
Enjoy your meal!	맛있게 드십시오!	man-nit-ge deu-sip-si-o!

waiter	웨이터	we-i-teo
waitress	웨이트리스	we-i-teu-ri-seu
bartender	바텐더	ba-ten-deo
menu	메뉴판	me-nyu-pan

spoon	숟가락	sut-ga-rak
knife	나이프	na-i-peu
fork	포크	po-keu
cup (e.g., coffee ~)	컵	keop

plate (dinner ~)	접시	jeop-si
saucer	받침 접시	bat-chim jeop-si

napkin (on table)	냅킨	naep-kin
toothpick	이쑤시개	i-ssu-si-gae

to order (meal)	주문하다	ju-mun-ha-da
course, dish	요리, 코스	yo-ri, ko-seu
portion	분량	bul-lyang
appetizer	애피타이저	ae-pi-ta-i-jeo

salad	샐러드	sael-leo-deu
soup	수프	su-peu

dessert	디저트	di-jeo-teu
jam (whole fruit jam)	잼	jaem
ice-cream	아이스크림	a-i-seu-keu-rim

check	계산서	gye-san-seo
to pay the check	계산하다	gye-san-ha-da
tip	팁	tip

13. House. Apartment. Part 1

house	집	jip
country house	시외 주택	si-oe ju-taek
villa (seaside ~)	별장	byeol-jang
floor, story	층	cheung
entrance	입구	ip-gu
wall	벽	byeok
roof	지붕	ji-bung
chimney	굴뚝	gul-ttuk
attic (storage place)	다락	da-rak
window	창문	chang-mun
window ledge	창가	chang-ga
balcony	발코니	bal-ko-ni
stairs (stairway)	계단	gye-dan
mailbox	우편함	u-pyeon-ham
garbage can	쓰레기통	sseu-re-gi-tong
elevator	엘리베이터	el-li-be-i-teo
electricity	전기	jeon-gi
light bulb	전구	jeon-gu
switch	스위치	seu-wi-chi
wall socket	소켓	so-ket
fuse	퓨즈	pyu-jeu
door	문	mun
handle, doorknob	손잡이	son-ja-bi
key	열쇠	yeol-soe
doormat	문 매트	mun mae-teu
door lock	자물쇠	ja-mul-soe
doorbell	벨	bel
knock (at the door)	노크	no-keu
to knock (vi)	두드리다	du-deu-ri-da
peephole	문구멍	mun-gu-meong
yard	마당	ma-dang
garden	정원	jeong-won
swimming pool	수영장	su-yeong-jang
gym (home gym)	헬스장	hel-seu-jang
tennis court	테니스장	te-ni-seu-jang
garage	차고	cha-go
private property	개인 소유물	gae-in so-yu-mul
warning sign	경고판	gyeong-go-pan
security	보안	bo-an
security guard	보안요원	bo-a-nyo-won
renovations	수리를	su-ri-reul
to renovate (vt)	수리를 하다	su-ri-reul ha-da

to put in order	정리하다	jeong-ni-ha-da
to paint (~ a wall)	페인트를 칠하다	pe-in-teu-reul chil-ha-da
wallpaper	벽지	byeok-ji
to varnish (vt)	니스를 칠하다	ni-seu-reul chil-ha-da
pipe	관, 파이프	gwan, pa-i-peu
tools	공구	gong-gu
basement	지하실	ji-ha-sil
sewerage (system)	하수도	ha-su-do

14. House. Apartment. Part 2

apartment	아파트	a-pa-teu
room	방	bang
bedroom	침실	chim-sil
dining room	식당	sik-dang
living room	거실	geo-sil
study (home office)	서재	seo-jae
entry room	곁방	gyeot-bang
bathroom (room with a bath or shower)	욕실	yok-sil
half bath	화장실	hwa-jang-sil
floor	마루	ma-ru
ceiling	천장	cheon-jang
to dust (vt)	먼지를 떨다	meon-ji-reul tteol-da
vacuum cleaner	진공 청소기	jin-gong cheong-so-gi
to vacuum (vt)	진공 청소기로 청소하다	jin-gong cheong-so-gi-ro cheong-so-ha-da
mop	대걸레	dae-geol-le
dust cloth	행주	haeng-ju
short broom	빗자루	bit-ja-ru
dustpan	쓰레받기	sseu-re-bat-gi
furniture	가구	ga-gu
table	식탁, 테이블	sik-tak, te-i-beul
chair	의자	ui-ja
armchair	안락 의자	al-lak gui-ja
bookcase	책장	chaek-jang
shelf	책꽂이	chaek-kko-ji
wardrobe	옷장	ot-jang
mirror	거울	geo-ul
carpet	양탄자	yang-tan-ja
fireplace	벽난로	byeong-nan-no
drapes	커튼	keo-teun

table lamp	테이블 램프	deung
chandelier	샹들리에	syang-deul-li-e
kitchen	부엌	bu-eok
gas stove (range)	가스 레인지	ga-seu re-in-ji
electric stove	전기 레인지	jeon-gi re-in-ji
microwave oven	전자 레인지	jeon-ja re-in-ji
refrigerator	냉장고	naeng-jang-go
freezer	냉동고	naeng-dong-go
dishwasher	식기 세척기	sik-gi se-cheok-gi
faucet	수도꼭지	su-do-kkok-ji
meat grinder	고기 분쇄기	go-gi bun-swae-gi
juicer	과즙기	gwa-jeup-gi
toaster	토스터	to-seu-teo
mixer	믹서기	mik-seo-gi
coffee machine	커피 메이커	keo-pi me-i-keo
kettle	주전자	ju-jeon-ja
teapot	티팟	ti-pat
TV set	텔레비전	tel-le-bi-jeon
VCR (video recorder)	비디오테이프 녹화기	bi-di-o-te-i-peu nok-wa-gi
iron (e.g., steam ~)	다리미	da-ri-mi
telephone	전화	jeon-hwa

15. Professions. Social status

director	사장	sa-jang
superior	상사	sang-sa
president	회장	hoe-jang
assistant	조수	jo-su
secretary	비서	bi-seo
owner, proprietor	소유자	so-yu-ja
partner	파트너	pa-teu-neo
stockholder	주주	ju-ju
businessman	사업가	sa-eop-ga
millionaire	백만장자	baeng-man-jang-ja
billionaire	억만장자	eong-man-jang-ja
actor	배우	bae-u
architect	건축가	geon-chuk-ga
banker	은행가	eun-haeng-ga
broker	브로커	beu-ro-keo
veterinarian	수의사	su-ui-sa
doctor	의사	ui-sa

chambermaid	객실 청소부	gaek-sil cheong-so-bu
designer	디자이너	di-ja-i-neo
correspondent	통신원	tong-sin-won
delivery man	배달원	bae-da-rwon
electrician	전기 기사	jeon-gi gi-sa
musician	음악가	eum-ak-ga
babysitter	애기보는 사람	ae-gi-bo-neun sa-ram
hairdresser	미용사	mi-yong-sa
herder, shepherd	목동	mok-dong
singer (masc.)	가수	ga-su
translator	번역가	beo-nyeok-ga
writer	작가	jak-ga
carpenter	목수	mok-su
cook	요리사	yo-ri-sa
fireman	소방관	so-bang-gwan
police officer	경찰관	gyeong-chal-gwan
mailman	우체부	u-che-bu
programmer	프로그래머	peu-ro-geu-rae-meo
salesman (store staff)	점원	jeom-won
worker	노동자	no-dong-ja
gardener	정원사	jeong-won-sa
plumber	배관공	bae-gwan-gong
dentist	치과 의사	chi-gwa ui-sa
flight attendant (fem.)	승무원	seung-mu-won
dancer (masc.)	무용가	mu-yong-ga
bodyguard	경호원	gyeong-ho-won
scientist	과학자	gwa-hak-ja
schoolteacher	선생님	seon-saeng-nim
farmer	농부	nong-bu
surgeon	외과 의사	oe-gwa ui-sa
miner	광부	gwang-bu
chef (kitchen chef)	주방장	ju-bang-jang
driver	운전 기사	un-jeon gi-sa

16. Sport

kind of sports	스포츠 종류	seu-po-cheu jong-nyu
soccer	축구	chuk-gu
hockey	하키	ha-ki
basketball	농구	nong-gu
baseball	야구	ya-gu
volleyball	배구	bae-gu
boxing	권투	gwon-tu

wrestling	레슬링	re-seul-ling
tennis	테니스	te-ni-seu
swimming	수영	su-yeong
chess	체스	che-seu
running	달리기	dal-li-gi
athletics	육상 경기	yuk-sang gyeong-gi
figure skating	피겨 스케이팅	pi-gyeo seu-ke-i-ting
cycling	자전거경기	ja-jeon-geo-gyeong-gi
billiards	당구	dang-gu
bodybuilding	보디빌딩	bo-di-bil-ding
golf	골프	gol-peu
scuba diving	스쿠버다이빙	seu-ku-beo-da-i-bing
sailing	요트타기	yo-teu-ta-gi
archery	양궁	yang-gung
period, half	경기 시간	gyeong-gi si-gan
half-time	하프 타임	ha-peu ta-im
tie	무승부	mu-seung-bu
to tie (vi)	무승부로 끝나다	mu-seung-bu-ro kkeun-na-da
treadmill	러닝 머신	reo-ning meo-sin
player	선수	seon-su
substitute	후보 선수	hu-bo seon-su
substitutes bench	후보 선수 대기석	hu-bo seon-su dae-gi-seok
match	경기	gyeong-gi
goal	골	gol
goalkeeper	골키퍼	gol-ki-peo
goal (score)	득점	deuk-jeom
Olympic Games	올림픽	ol-lim-pik
to set a record	기록을 세우다	gi-ro-geul se-u-da
final	결승전	gyeol-seung-jeon
champion	챔피언	chaem-pi-eon
championship	선수권	seon-su-gwon
winner	승리자	seung-ni-ja
victory	승리	seung-ni
to win (vi)	이기다	i-gi-da
to lose (not win)	지다	ji-da
medal	메달	me-dal
first place	일등	il-deung
second place	준우승	seu-ko-eo-bo-deu
third place	3위	sam-wi
stadium	경기장	gyeong-gi-jang
fan, supporter	서포터	seo-po-teo
trainer, coach	코치	ko-chi
training	훈련	hul-lyeon

17. Foreign languages. Orthography

language	언어	eon-eo
to study (vt)	공부하다	gong-bu-ha-da
pronunciation	발음	ba-reum
accent	악센트	ak-sen-teu
noun	명사	myeong-sa
adjective	형용사	hyeong-yong-sa
verb	동사	dong-sa
adverb	부사	bu-sa
pronoun	대명사	dae-myeong-sa
interjection	감탄사	gam-tan-sa
preposition	전치사	jeon-chi-sa
root	어근	eo-geun
ending	어미	eo-mi
prefix	접두사	jeop-du-sa
syllable	음절	eum-jeol
suffix	접미사	jeom-mi-sa
stress mark	강세	gang-se
period, dot	마침표	ma-chim-pyo
comma	쉼표	swim-pyo
colon	콜론	kol-lon
ellipsis	말줄임표	mal-ju-rim-pyo
question	질문	jil-mun
question mark	물음표	mu-reum-pyo
exclamation point	느낌표	neu-kkim-pyo
in quotation marks	따옴표 안에	tta-om-pyo a-ne
in parenthesis	괄호 속에	gwal-ho so-ge
letter	글자	geul-ja
capital letter	대문자	dae-mun-ja
sentence	문장	mun-jang
group of words	문구	mun-gu
expression	표현	pyo-hyeon
subject	주어	ju-eo
predicate	서술어	seo-su-reo
line	줄	jul
paragraph	단락	dal-lak
synonym	동의어	dong-ui-eo
antonym	반의어	ban-ui-eo
exception	예외	ye-oe
to underline (vt)	밑줄을 긋다	mit-ju-reul geut-da
rules	규칙	gyu-chik

grammar	문법	mun-beop
vocabulary	어휘	eo-hwi
phonetics	음성학	eum-seong-hak
alphabet	알파벳	al-pa-bet

textbook	교과서	gyo-gwa-seo
dictionary	사전	sa-jeon
phrasebook	회화집	hoe-hwa-jip

word	단어	dan-eo
meaning	의미	ui-mi
memory	기억력	gi-eong-nyeok

18. The Earth. Geography

the Earth	지구	ji-gu
the globe (the Earth)	지구	ji-gu
planet	행성	haeng-seong

geography	지리학	ji-ri-hak
nature	자연	ja-yeon
map	지도	ji-do
atlas	지도첩	ji-do-cheop

in the north	북쪽에	buk-jjo-ge
in the south	남쪽에	nam-jjo-ge
in the west	서쪽에	seo-jjo-ge
in the east	동쪽에	dong-jjo-ge

sea	바다	ba-da
ocean	대양	dae-yang
gulf (bay)	만	man
straits	해협	hae-hyeop

continent (mainland)	대륙	dae-ryuk
island	섬	seom
peninsula	반도	ban-do
archipelago	군도	gun-do

harbor	항구	hang-gu
coral reef	산호초	san-ho-cho
shore	해변	hae-byeon
coast	바닷가	ba-dat-ga

flow (flood tide)	밀물	mil-mul
ebb (ebb tide)	썰물	sseol-mul

latitude	위도	wi-do
longitude	경도	gyeong-do
parallel	위도선	wi-do-seon

equator	적도	jeok-do
sky	하늘	ha-neul
horizon	수평선	su-pyeong-seon
atmosphere	대기	dae-gi
mountain	산	san
summit, top	정상	jeong-sang
cliff	절벽	jeol-byeok
hill	언덕, 작은 산	eon-deok, ja-geun san
volcano	화산	hwa-san
glacier	빙하	bing-ha
waterfall	폭포	pok-po
plain	평원	pyeong-won
river	강	gang
spring (natural source)	샘	saem
bank (of river)	둑	duk
downstream (adv)	하류로	gang ha-ryu-ro
upstream (adv)	상류로	sang-nyu-ro
lake	호수	ho-su
dam	댐	daem
canal	운하	un-ha
swamp (marshland)	늪, 소택지	neup, so-taek-ji
ice	얼음	eo-reum

19. Countries of the world. Part 1

Europe	유럽	yu-reop
European Union	유럽 연합	yu-reop byeon-hap
European (n)	유럽 사람	yu-reop sa-ram
European (adj)	유럽의	yu-reo-bui
Austria	오스트리아	o-seu-teu-ri-a
Great Britain	영국	yeong-guk
England	잉글랜드	ing-geul-laen-deu
Belgium	벨기에	bel-gi-e
Germany	독일	do-gil
Netherlands	네덜란드	ne-deol-lan-deu
Holland	네덜란드	ne-deol-lan-deu
Greece	그리스	geu-ri-seu
Denmark	덴마크	den-ma-keu
Ireland	아일랜드	a-il-laen-deu
Iceland	아이슬란드	a-i-seul-lan-deu
Spain	스페인	seu-pe-in
Italy	이탈리아	i-tal-li-a
Cyprus	키프로스	ki-peu-ro-seu

Malta	몰타	mol-ta
Norway	노르웨이	no-reu-we-i
Portugal	포르투갈	po-reu-tu-gal
Finland	핀란드	pil-lan-deu
France	프랑스	peu-rang-seu
Sweden	스웨덴	seu-we-den
Switzerland	스위스	seu-wi-seu
Scotland	스코틀랜드	seu-ko-teul-laen-deu
Vatican	바티칸	ba-ti-kan
Liechtenstein	리히텐슈타인	ri-hi-ten-syu-ta-in
Luxembourg	룩셈부르크	ruk-sem-bu-reu-keu
Monaco	모나코	mo-na-ko
Albania	알바니아	al-ba-ni-a
Bulgaria	불가리아	bul-ga-ri-a
Hungary	헝가리	heong-ga-ri
Latvia	라트비아	ra-teu-bi-a
Lithuania	리투아니아	ri-tu-a-ni-a
Poland	폴란드	pol-lan-deu
Romania	루마니아	ru-ma-ni-a
Serbia	세르비아	se-reu-bi-a
Slovakia	슬로바키아	seul-lo-ba-ki-a
Croatia	크로아티아	keu-ro-a-ti-a
Czech Republic	체코	che-ko
Estonia	에스토니아	e-seu-to-ni-a
Bosnia and Herzegovina	보스니아 헤르체코비나	bo-seu-ni-a he-reu-che-ko-bi-na
Macedonia (Republic of ~)	마케도니아	ma-ke-do-ni-a
Slovenia	슬로베니아	seul-lo-be-ni-a
Montenegro	몬테네그로	mon-te-ne-geu-ro
Belarus	벨로루시	bel-lo-ru-si
Moldova, Moldavia	몰도바	mol-do-ba
Russia	러시아	reo-si-a
Ukraine	우크라이나	u-keu-ra-i-na

20. Countries of the world. Part 2

Asia	아시아	a-si-a
Vietnam	베트남	be-teu-nam
India	인도	in-do
Israel	이스라엘	i-seu-ra-el
China	중국	jung-guk
Lebanon	레바논	re-ba-non
Mongolia	몽골	mong-gol
Malaysia	말레이시아	mal-le-i-si-a

Pakistan	파키스탄	pa-ki-seu-tan
Saudi Arabia	사우디아라비아	sa-u-di-a-ra-bi-a

Thailand	태국	tae-guk
Taiwan	대만	dae-man
Turkey	터키	teo-ki
Japan	일본	il-bon
Afghanistan	아프가니스탄	a-peu-ga-ni-seu-tan

Bangladesh	방글라데시	bang-geul-la-de-si
Indonesia	인도네시아	in-do-ne-si-a
Jordan	요르단	yo-reu-dan
Iraq	이라크	i-ra-keu
Iran	이란	i-ran

Cambodia	캄보디아	kam-bo-di-a
Kuwait	쿠웨이트	ku-we-i-teu
Laos	라오스	ra-o-seu
Myanmar	미얀마	mi-yan-ma
Nepal	네팔	ne-pal

United Arab Emirates	아랍에미리트	a-ra-be-mi-ri-teu
Syria	시리아	si-ri-a
Palestine	팔레스타인	pal-le-seu-ta-in
South Korea	한국	han-guk
North Korea	북한	buk-an

United States of America	미국	mi-guk
Canada	캐나다	kae-na-da
Mexico	멕시코	mek-si-ko
Argentina	아르헨티나	a-reu-hen-ti-na
Brazil	브라질	beu-ra-jil

Colombia	콜롬비아	kol-lom-bi-a
Cuba	쿠바	ku-ba
Chile	칠레	chil-le
Venezuela	베네수엘라	be-ne-su-el-la
Ecuador	에콰도르	e-kwa-do-reu

The Bahamas	바하마	ba-ha-ma
Panama	파나마	pa-na-ma
Egypt	이집트	i-jip-teu

Morocco	모로코	mo-ro-ko
Tunisia	튀니지	twi-ni-ji

Kenya	케냐	ke-nya
Libya	리비아	ri-bi-a
South Africa	남아프리카 공화국	nam-a-peu-ri-ka gong-hwa-guk

Australia	호주	ho-ju
New Zealand	뉴질랜드	nyu-jil-laen-deu

21. Weather. Natural disasters

weather	날씨	nal-ssi
weather forecast	일기 예보	il-gi ye-bo
temperature	온도	on-do
thermometer	온도계	on-do-gye
barometer	기압계	gi-ap-gye
sun	해	hae
to shine (vi)	빛나다	bin-na-da
sunny (day)	화창한	hwa-chang-han
to come up (vi)	뜨다	tteu-da
to set (vi)	지다	ji-da
rain	비	bi
it's raining	비가 오다	bi-ga o-da
pouring rain	억수	eok-su
puddle	웅덩이	ung-deong-i
to get wet (in rain)	젖다	jeot-da
thunderstorm	뇌우	noe-u
lightning (~ strike)	번개	beon-gae
to flash (vi)	번쩍이다	beon-jjeo-gi-da
thunder	천둥	cheon-dung
it's thundering	천둥이 치다	cheon-dung-i chi-da
hail	싸락눈	ssa-rang-nun
it's hailing	싸락눈이 내리다	ssa-rang-nun-i nae-ri-da
heat (extreme ~)	더위	deo-wi
it's hot	덥다	deop-da
it's warm	따뜻하다	tta-tteu-ta-da
it's cold	춥다	chup-da
fog (mist)	안개	an-gae
foggy	안개가 자욱한	an-gae-ga ja-uk-an
cloud	구름	gu-reum
cloudy (adj)	구름의	gu-reum-ui
humidity	습합, 습기	seu-pam, seup-gi
snow	눈	nun
it's snowing	눈이 오다	nun-i o-da
frost (severe ~, freezing cold)	지독한 서리	ji-dok-an seo-ri
below zero (adv)	영하	yeong-ha
hoarfrost	서리	seo-ri
disaster	재해	jae-hae
flood, inundation	홍수	hong-su
avalanche	눈사태	nun-sa-tae
earthquake	지진	ji-jin
tremor, quake	진동	jin-dong

epicenter	진앙	jin-ang
eruption	폭발	pok-bal
lava	용암	yong-am

tornado	토네이도	to-ne-i-do
twister	회오리바람	hoe-o-ri-ba-ram
hurricane	허리케인	heo-ri-ke-in
tsunami	해일	hae-il

22. Animals. Part 1

| animal | 동물 | dong-mul |
| predator | 육식 동물 | yuk-sik dong-mul |

tiger	호랑이	ho-rang-i
lion	사자	sa-ja
wolf	이리	i-ri
fox	여우	yeo-u
jaguar	재규어	jae-gyu-eo

lynx	스라소니	seu-ra-so-ni
coyote	코요테	ko-yo-te
jackal	재칼	jae-kal
hyena	하이에나	ha-i-e-na

squirrel	다람쥐	da-ram-jwi
hedgehog	고슴도치	go-seum-do-chi
rabbit	굴토끼	gul-to-kki
raccoon	너구리	neo-gu-ri

hamster	햄스터	haem-seu-teo
mole	두더지	du-deo-ji
mouse	생쥐	saeng-jwi
rat	시궁쥐	si-gung-jwi
bat	박쥐	bak-jwi

beaver	비버	bi-beo
horse	말	mal
deer	사슴	sa-seum
camel	낙타	nak-ta
zebra	얼룩말	eol-lung-mal

whale	고래	go-rae
seal	바다표범	ba-da-pyo-beom
walrus	바다코끼리	ba-da-ko-kki-ri
dolphin	돌고래	dol-go-rae

bear	곰	gom
monkey	원숭이	won-sung-i
elephant	코끼리	ko-kki-ri

rhinoceros	코뿔소	ko-ppul-so
giraffe	기린	gi-rin
hippopotamus	하마	ha-ma
kangaroo	캥거루	kaeng-geo-ru
cat	고양이	go-yang-i
cow	암소	am-so
bull	황소	hwang-so
sheep (ewe)	양, 암양	yang, a-myang
goat	염소	yeom-so
donkey	당나귀	dang-na-gwi
pig, hog	돼지	dwae-ji
hen (chicken)	암탉	am-tak
rooster	수탉	su-tak
duck	집오리	ji-bo-ri
goose	집거위	jip-geo-wi
turkey (hen)	칠면조	chil-myeon-jo
sheepdog	양치기 개	yang-chi-gi gae

23. Animals. Part 2

bird	새	sae
pigeon	비둘기	bi-dul-gi
sparrow	참새	cham-sae
tit (great tit)	박새	bak-sae
magpie	까치	kka-chi
eagle	독수리	dok-su-ri
hawk	매	mae
falcon	매	mae
swan	백조	baek-jo
crane	두루미	du-ru-mi
stork	황새	hwang-sae
parrot	앵무새	aeng-mu-sae
peacock	공작	gong-jak
ostrich	타조	ta-jo
heron	왜가리	wae-ga-ri
nightingale	나이팅게일	na-i-ting-ge-il
swallow	제비	je-bi
woodpecker	딱따구리	ttak-tta-gu-ri
cuckoo	뻐꾸기	ppeo-kku-gi
owl	올빼미	ol-ppae-mi
penguin	펭귄	peng-gwin
tuna	참치	cham-chi

trout	송어	song-eo
eel	뱀장어	baem-jang-eo
shark	상어	sang-eo
crab	게	ge
jellyfish	해파리	hae-pa-ri
octopus	낙지	nak-ji
starfish	불가사리	bul-ga-sa-ri
sea urchin	성게	seong-ge
seahorse	해마	hae-ma
shrimp	새우	sae-u
snake	뱀	baem
viper	살무사	sal-mu-sa
lizard	도마뱀	do-ma-baem
iguana	이구아나	i-gu-a-na
chameleon	카멜레온	ka-mel-le-on
scorpion	전갈	jeon-gal
turtle	거북	geo-buk
frog	개구리	gae-gu-ri
crocodile	악어	a-geo
insect, bug	곤충	gon-chung
butterfly	나비	na-bi
ant	개미	gae-mi
fly	파리	pa-ri
mosquito	모기	mo-gi
beetle	딱정벌레	ttak-jeong-beol-le
bee	꿀벌	kkul-beol
spider	거미	geo-mi

24. Trees. Plants

tree	나무	na-mu
birch	자작나무	ja-jang-na-mu
oak	오크	o-keu
linden tree	보리수	bo-ri-su
aspen	사시나무	sa-si-na-mu
maple	단풍나무	dan-pung-na-mu
spruce	가문비나무	ga-mun-bi-na-mu
pine	소나무	so-na-mu
cedar	시다	si-da
poplar	포플러	po-peul-leo
rowan	마가목	ma-ga-mok
beech	너도밤나무	neo-do-bam-na-mu

elm	느릅나무	neu-reum-na-mu
ash (tree)	물푸레나무	mul-pu-re-na-mu
chestnut	밤나무	bam-na-mu
palm tree	야자나무	ya-ja-na-mu
bush	덤불	deom-bul
mushroom	버섯	beo-seot
poisonous mushroom	독버섯	dok-beo-seot
russula	무당버섯	mu-dang-beo-seot
fly agaric	광대버섯	gwang-dae-beo-seot
death cap	알광대버섯	al-gwang-dae-beo-seot
flower	꽃	kkot
bouquet (of flowers)	꽃다발	kkot-da-bal
rose (flower)	장미	jang-mi
tulip	튤립	tyul-lip
carnation	카네이션	ka-ne-i-syeon
camomile	캐모마일	kae-mo-ma-il
cactus	선인장	seon-in-jang
lily of the valley	은방울꽃	eun-bang-ul-kkot
snowdrop	스노드롭	seu-no-deu-rop
water lily	수련	su-ryeon
greenhouse (tropical ~)	온실	on-sil
lawn	잔디	jan-di
flowerbed	꽃밭	kkot-bat
plant	식물	sing-mul
grass	풀	pul
leaf	잎	ip
petal	꽃잎	kko-chip
stem	줄기	jul-gi
young plant (shoot)	새싹	sae-ssak
cereal crops	곡류	gong-nyu
wheat	밀	mil
rye	호밀	ho-mil
oats	귀리	gwi-ri
millet	수수, 기장	su-su, gi-jang
barley	보리	bo-ri
corn	옥수수	ok-su-su
rice	쌀	ssal

25. Various useful words

balance (of situation)	균형	gyun-hyeong
base (basis)	근거	geun-geo
beginning	시작	si-jak

category	범주	beom-ju
choice	선택	seon-taek
coincidence	우연	u-yeon
comparison	비교	bi-gyo
degree (extent, amount)	정도	jeong-do

development	개발	gae-bal
difference	다름	da-reum
effect (e.g., of drugs)	효과	hyo-gwa
effort (exertion)	노력	no-ryeok

element	요소	yo-so
example (illustration)	예	ye
fact	사실	sa-sil
help	도움	do-um

ideal	이상	i-sang
kind (sort, type)	종류	jong-nyu
mistake, error	실수	sil-su
moment	순간	sun-gan

obstacle	장애	jang-ae
part (~ of sth)	부분	bu-bun
pause (break)	휴식	hyu-sik
position	위치	wi-chi

problem	문제	mun-je
process	과정	gwa-jeong
progress	진척	jin-cheok
property (quality)	특질	teuk-jil

reaction	반응	ba-neung
risk	위험	wi-heom
secret	비밀	bi-mil
series	일련	il-lyeon

shape (outer form)	모양	mo-yang
situation	상황	sang-hwang
solution	해결	hae-gyeol
standard (adj)	기준의	gi-jun-ui

stop (pause)	정지	jeong-ji
style	스타일	seu-ta-il
system	체계	che-gye
table (chart)	표	pyo
tempo, rate	완급	wan-geup

term (word, expression)	용어	yong-eo
truth (e.g., moment of ~)	진리	jil-li
turn (please wait your ~)	차례	cha-rye
urgent (adj)	긴급한	gin-geu-pan

utility (usefulness)	유용성	yu-yong-seong
variant (alternative)	변종	byeon-jong
way (means, method)	방법	bang-beop
zone	지대	ji-dae

26. Modifiers. Adjectives. Part 1

additional (adj)	추가의	chu-ga-ui
ancient (~ civilization)	고대의	go-dae-ui
artificial (adj)	인공의	in-gong-ui
bad (adj)	나쁜	na-ppeun
beautiful (person)	아름다운	a-reum-da-un
big (in size)	큰	keun
bitter (taste)	쓴	sseun
blind (sightless)	눈먼	nun-meon
central (adj)	중앙의	jung-ang-ui
children's (adj)	어린이의	eo-ri-ni-ui
clandestine (secret)	은밀한	eun-mil-han
clean (free from dirt)	깨끗한	kkae-kkeu-tan
clever (smart)	영리한	yeong-ni-han
compatible (adj)	호환이 되는	ho-hwan-i doe-neun
contented (satisfied)	만족한	man-jok-an
dangerous (adj)	위험한	wi-heom-han
dead (not alive)	죽은	ju-geun
dense (fog, smoke)	밀집한	mil-ji-pan
difficult (decision)	어려운	eo-ryeo-un
dirty (not clean)	더러운	deo-reo-un
easy (not difficult)	쉬운	swi-un
empty (glass, room)	빈	bin
exact (amount)	정확한	jeong-hwak-an
excellent (adj)	우수한	u-su-han
excessive (adj)	과도한	gwa-do-han
exterior (adj)	외부의	oe-bu-ui
fast (quick)	빠른	ppa-reun
fertile (land, soil)	비옥한	bi-ok-an
fragile (china, glass)	깨지기 쉬운	kkae-ji-gi swi-un
free (at no cost)	무료의	mu-ryo-ui
fresh (~ water)	민물의	min-mu-rui
frozen (food)	언	naeng-dong-doen
full (completely filled)	가득 찬	ga-deuk chan
happy (adj)	행복한	haeng-bok-an
hard (not soft)	단단한	dan-dan-han
huge (adj)	거대한	geo-dae-han

ill (sick, unwell)	병든	byeong-deun
immobile (adj)	동요되지 않는	dong-yo-doe-ji an-neun
important (adj)	중요한	jung-yo-han

interior (adj)	내부의	nae-bu-ui
last (e.g., ~ week)	지난	ji-nan
last (final)	마지막의	ma-ji-ma-gui
left (e.g., ~ side)	왼쪽의	oen-jjo-gui
legal (legitimate)	합법적인	hap-beop-jeo-gin

light (in weight)	가벼운	ga-byeo-un
liquid (fluid)	액체의	aek-che-ui
long (e.g., ~ hair)	긴	gin
loud (voice, etc.)	시끄러운	si-kkeu-reo-un
low (voice)	낮은	na-jeun

27. Modifiers. Adjectives. Part 2

main (principal)	주요한	ju-yo-han
matt, matte	무광의	mu-gwang-ui
mysterious (adj)	신비한	sin-bi-han
narrow (street, etc.)	좁은	jo-beun
native (~ country)	태어난 곳의	tae-eo-nan gos-ui

negative (~ response)	부정적인	bu-jeong-jeo-gin
new (adj)	새로운	sae-ro-un
next (e.g., ~ week)	다음의	da-eum-ui
normal (adj)	평범한	pyeong-beom-han
not difficult (adj)	힘들지 않은	him-deul-ji a-neun

obligatory (adj)	의무적인	ui-mu-jeo-gin
old (house)	오래된	o-rae-doen
open (adj)	열린	yeol-lin
opposite (adj)	반대의	ban-dae-ui
ordinary (usual)	보통의	bo-tong-ui

original (unusual)	독창적인	dok-chang-jeo-gin
personal (adj)	개인의	gae-in-ui
polite (adj)	공손한	gong-son-han
poor (not rich)	가난한	ga-nan-han

possible (adj)	가능한	ga-neung-han
principal (main)	주요한	ju-yo-han
probable (adj)	개연성 있는	gae-yeon-seong in-neun
prolonged (e.g., ~ applause)	장기적인	jang-gi-jeo-gin
public (open to all)	공공의	gong-gong-ui

| rare (adj) | 드문 | deu-mun |
| raw (uncooked) | 날것의 | nal-geos-ui |

right (not left)	오른쪽의	o-reun-jjo-gui
ripe (fruit)	익은	i-geun
risky (adj)	위험한	wi-heom-han
sad (~ look)	슬픈	seul-peun
second hand (adj)	중고의	jung-go-ui
shallow (water)	얕은	ya-teun
sharp (blade, etc.)	날카로운	nal-ka-ro-un
short (in length)	짧은	jjal-beun
similar (adj)	비슷한	bi-seu-tan
small (in size)	작은	ja-geun
smooth (surface)	매끈한	mae-kkeun-han
soft (~ toys)	부드러운	bu-deu-reo-un
solid (~ wall)	튼튼한	teun-teun-han
sour (flavor, taste)	시큼한	si-keum-han
spacious (house, etc.)	넓은	neol-beun
special (adj)	특별한	teuk-byeol-han
straight (line, road)	곧은	go-deun
strong (person)	강한	gang-han
stupid (foolish)	미련한	mi-ryeon-han
superb, perfect (adj)	우수한, 완벽한	u-su-han, wan-byeok-an
sweet (sugary)	단	dan
tan (adj)	햇볕에 탄	haet-byeo-te tan
tasty (delicious)	맛있는	man-nin-neun
unclear (adj)	불분명한	bul-bun-myeong-han

28. Verbs. Part 1

to accuse (vt)	비난하다	bi-nan-ha-da
to agree (say yes)	동의하다	dong-ui-ha-da
to announce (vt)	알리다	al-li-da
to answer (vi, vt)	대답하다	dae-da-pa-da
to apologize (vi)	사과하다	sa-gwa-ha-da
to arrive (vi)	도착하다	do-chak-a-da
to ask (~ oneself)	묻다	mut-da
to be absent	결석하다	gyeol-seok-a-da
to be afraid	무서워하다	mu-seo-wo-ha-da
to be born	태어나다	tae-eo-na-da
to be in a hurry	서두르다	seo-du-reu-da
to beat (to hit)	때리다	ttae-ri-da
to begin (vt)	시작하다	si-jak-a-da
to believe (in God)	믿다	mit-da
to belong to ...	... 에 속하다	... e sok-a-da
to break (split into pieces)	깨뜨리다	kkae-tteu-ri-da

to build (vt)	건설하다	geon-seol-ha-da
to buy (purchase)	사다	sa-da
can (v aux)	할 수 있다	hal su it-da
can (v aux)	할 수 있다	hal su it-da
to cancel (call off)	취소하다	chwi-so-ha-da
to catch (vt)	잡다	jap-da
to change (vt)	바꾸다	ba-kku-da
to check (to examine)	확인하다	hwa-gin-ha-da
to choose (select)	선택하다	seon-taek-a-da
to clean up (tidy)	청소하다	cheong-so-ha-da
to close (vt)	닫다	dat-da
to compare (vt)	비교하다	bi-gyo-ha-da
to complain (vi, vt)	불평하다	bul-pyeong-ha-da
to confirm (vt)	확인해 주다	hwa-gin-hae ju-da
to congratulate (vt)	축하하다	chuk-a-ha-da
to cook (dinner)	요리하다	yo-ri-ha-da
to copy (vt)	복사하다	bok-sa-ha-da
to cost (vt)	값이 … 이다	gap-si … i-da
to count (add up)	세다	se-da
to count on …	… 에 의지하다	… e ui-ji-ha-da
to create (vt)	창조하다	chang-jo-ha-da
to cry (weep)	울다	ul-da
to dance (vi, vt)	춤추다	chum-chu-da
to deceive (vi, vt)	속이다	so-gi-da
to decide (~ to do sth)	결심하다	gyeol-sim-ha-da
to delete (vt)	삭제하다	sak-je-ha-da
to demand (request firmly)	요구하다	yo-gu-ha-da
to deny (vt)	거부하다	geo-bu-ha-da
to depend on …	… 을 신뢰하다	… seul sil-loe-ha-da
to despise (vt)	경멸하다	gyeong-myeol-ha-da
to die (vi)	죽다	juk-da
to dig (vt)	파다	pa-da
to disappear (vi)	사라지다	sa-ra-ji-da
to discuss (vt)	의논하다	ui-non-ha-da
to disturb (vt)	방해하다	bang-hae-ha-da

29. Verbs. Part 2

to dive (vi)	잠수하다	jam-su-ha-da
to divorce (vi)	이혼하다	i-hon-ha-da
to do (vt)	하다	ha-da
to doubt (have doubts)	의심하다	ui-sim-ha-da
to drink (vi, vt)	마시다	ma-si-da
to drop (let fall)	떨어뜨리다	tteo-reo-tteu-ri-da

to dry (clothes, hair)	말리다	mal-li-da
to eat (vi, vt)	먹다	meok-da
to end (~ a relationship)	끝내다	kkeun-nae-da
to excuse (forgive)	용서하다	yong-seo-ha-da
to exist (vi)	존재하다	jon-jae-ha-da
to expect (foresee)	예상하다	ye-sang-ha-da
to explain (vt)	설명하다	seol-myeong-ha-da
to fall (vi)	떨어지다	tteo-reo-ji-da
to fight (street fight, etc.)	싸우다	ssa-u-da
to find (vt)	찾다	chat-da
to finish (vt)	끝내다	kkeun-nae-da
to fly (vi)	날다	nal-da
to forbid (vt)	금지하다	geum-ji-ha-da
to forget (vi, vt)	잊다	it-da
to forgive (vt)	용서하다	yong-seo-ha-da
to get tired	피곤하다	pi-gon-ha-da
to give (vt)	주다	ju-da
to go (on foot)	가다	ga-da
to hate (vt)	증오하다	jeung-o-ha-da
to have (vt)	가지다	ga-ji-da
to have breakfast	아침을 먹다	a-chi-meul meok-da
to have dinner	저녁을 먹다	jeo-nyeo-geul meok-da
to have lunch	점심을 먹다	jeom-si-meul meok-da
to hear (vt)	듣다	deut-da
to help (vt)	도와주다	do-wa-ju-da
to hide (vt)	숨기다	sum-gi-da
to hope (vi, vt)	희망하다	hui-mang-ha-da
to hunt (vi, vt)	사냥하다	sa-nyang-ha-da
to hurry (vi)	서두르다	seo-du-reu-da
to insist (vi, vt)	주장하다	ju-jang-ha-da
to insult (vt)	모욕하다	mo-yok-a-da
to invite (vt)	초대하다	cho-dae-ha-da
to joke (vi)	농담하다	nong-dam-ha-da
to keep (vt)	보관하다	bo-gwan-ha-da
to kill (vt)	죽이다	ju-gi-da
to know (sb)	알다	al-da
to know (sth)	알다	al-da
to like (I like …)	좋아하다	jo-a-ha-da
to look at …	… 를 보다	… reul bo-da
to lose (umbrella, etc.)	잃어버리다	i-reo-beo-ri-da
to love (sb)	사랑하다	sa-rang-ha-da
to make a mistake	실수하다	sil-su-ha-da
to meet (vi, vt)	만나다	man-na-da
to miss (school, etc.)	결석하다	gyeol-seok-a-da

30. Verbs. Part 3

to obey (vi, vt)	복종하다	bok-jong-ha-da
to open (vt)	열다	yeol-da
to participate (vi)	참가하다	cham-ga-ha-da
to pay (vi, vt)	지불하다	ji-bul-ha-da
to permit (vt)	허락하다	heo-rak-a-da
to play (children)	놀다	nol-da
to pray (vi, vt)	기도하다	gi-do-ha-da
to promise (vt)	약속하다	yak-sok-a-da
to propose (vt)	제안하다	je-an-ha-da
to prove (vt)	증명하다	jeung-myeong-ha-da
to read (vi, vt)	읽다	ik-da
to receive (vt)	받다	bat-da
to rent (sth from sb)	임대하다	im-dae-ha-da
to repeat (say again)	반복하다	ban-bok-a-da
to reserve, to book	예약하다	ye-yak-a-da
to run (vi)	달리다	dal-li-da
to save (rescue)	구조하다	gu-jo-ha-da
to say (~ thank you)	말하다	mal-ha-da
to see (vt)	보다	bo-da
to sell (vt)	팔다	pal-da
to send (vt)	보내다	bo-nae-da
to shoot (vi)	쏘다	sso-da
to shout (vi)	소리치다	so-ri-chi-da
to show (vt)	보여주다	bo-yeo-ju-da
to sign (document)	서명하다	seo-myeong-ha-da
to sing (vi)	노래하다	no-rae-ha-da
to sit down (vi)	앉다	an-da
to smile (vi)	미소를 짓다	mi-so-reul jit-da
to speak (vi, vt)	말하다	mal-ha-da
to steal (money, etc.)	훔치다	hum-chi-da
to stop (please ~ calling me)	그만두다	geu-man-du-da
to study (vt)	공부하다	gong-bu-ha-da
to swim (vi)	수영하다	su-yeong-ha-da
to take (vt)	잡다	jap-da
to talk to ...	… 와 말하다	… wa mal-ha-da
to tell (story, joke)	이야기하다	i-ya-gi-ha-da
to thank (vt)	감사하다	gam-sa-ha-da
to think (vi, vt)	생각하다	saeng-gak-a-da
to translate (vt)	번역하다	beo-nyeok-a-da
to trust (vt)	신뢰하다	sil-loe-ha-da
to try (attempt)	해보다	hae-bo-da

to turn (e.g., ~ left)	돌다	dol-da
to turn off	끄다	kkeu-da
to turn on	켜다	kyeo-da
to understand (vt)	이해하다	i-hae-ha-da
to wait (vt)	기다리다	gi-da-ri-da
to want (wish, desire)	원하다	won-ha-da
to work (vi)	일하다	il-ha-da
to write (vt)	쓰다	sseu-da